S0-AXL-371

Dead End Bluff

DEAD END BLUFF

Elizabeth Witheridge

DRAWINGS BY CHARLES GEER

Atheneum   1966   New York

ACKNOWLEDGMENTS

DR. EVELYN DENO, head of Special Education in the Minneapolis Public Schools, who made it possible for me to visit freely and observe blind children participating in the excellent program for them in the public schools.

MRS. JOHN OLMSCHEID and MRS. DAVID THIES, resource teachers of blind children, who welcomed me to their classrooms for many weeks of observation, and shared their philosophy of education for blind children with me. Both of them also gave invaluable help in their criticism of the manuscript.

MR. and MRS. A. WELLS PECK, owners of the Pitch Road Kennels, Litchfield, Connecticut, who so graciously permitted use of their kennel name in the book and contributed valuable material on the Norwegian elkhound.

THE CHILDREN OF CALHOUN ELEMENTARY and SUSAN B. ANTHONY JUNIOR HIGH SCHOOLS who were trained in the program for the blind and let me be their friend.

In memory of
PROFESSOR HELEN RANDOLPH EMMONS
who spent her life for children

Dead End Bluff

Chapter 1

"THIS WAY, QUIG! OVER THIS WAY . . . FASTER!
This way!"

Quig's strokes slashed through the water, clean
and sure. He put on a burst of speed, trying to follow the sound of his friends' voices on the raft.

"You turned too far! You're going to hit Peg . . .
That's better. You're gonna make it!" They kept
up a constant chatter.

Quig buried his head in the cold water and surged
ahead. This time he was going to win. He was going
to beat Peg Bradford, who always won their races.
Today he was doing it!

"This way, Quig," his friends screamed. "You've
done it!—Oh-hhhhh!"

Their triumphant yell plummeted downward like a fizzling skyrocket on the Fourth of July, and Quig knew he had missed again. Hands reached out for him and pulled him dripping onto the raft.

"How far off was I?" he demanded.

"Not more than a foot," moaned Joe. "We shouldn't have let you turn so far. You had her beat, but you just missed the raft at the last minute."

Jefferson Quigley Smith, third in his family with the same unusual name, shook the water out of his ears and sat with a puzzled frown on his face.

"Can't see why," he said finally, almost to himself. "I do it every time. Certainly no point in my entering the Midsummer Meet if I can't find the raft."

"You almost did it today, Quig." It was Peg's voice, close to him. "I was sure you were going to hit it. You were a whole length ahead of me. Then you veered and overshot it. I think you're afraid of hitting your head on the raft."

"Afraid!" Quig ground out the word furiously. He flushed an angry red under his tan. "I am not afraid. Just get that right out of your head. I'm not afraid of anything!"

"I knew it would make you mad," Peg answered calmly, "but I still think that's the trouble. My goodness, it's nothing in the least to be ashamed of. I would be afraid of bashing my head on the raft,

4

too, if I couldn't see it."

Quig's flush died away and he stretched out in the sun, relaxing his tensed muscles. "Maybe you're right, Peg," he said slowly. "I don't believe I'm afraid of hitting my head, but that could be it, I s'pose. I really think, though, that I just don't listen carefully enough. My 'radar' seems to quit working when I'm excited."

"Well, whatever's wrong, you've got to get over it. You're the best we've got to win the free style," Don announced firmly.

"Yeah," said Mike. "I'm no good at free style. Don's too slow. Peg's fast but she hasn't got the strength to go the hundred yards at top speed. It's you or nothin' to beat the kids from Green Valley and bring that trophy home again."

"You've got a couple of months, Quig," Joe reminded him. "It's only the first of June. Come on— race you back."

"Wait a minute, Quig. I'm comin' out," came a yell from shore. "Betcha I can swim out to the raft just as fast as you can. Here I come!"

Quig recognized his little brother's voice.

"Don't you dare come out here, Tommy!" he yelled. "It's way over your head."

He heard a splash as Tommy jumped into the water. "That kid's going to drown himself some day," Quig grumbled as he dived off the raft. He

5

swam under water, listening for Tommy's churning dog paddle. In a minute he came up under the boy and grabbed his thrashing feet.

"Hey!" squeaked Tommy, gurgling as he went under.

"Hey, yourself," Quig said, surfacing with a firm grip on Tommy's trunks.

He struck out for the narrow strip of beach with his brother tucked securely under his arm.

"Gee!" cried Peggy admiringly as she caught up with him. "I'd give anything to be able to do that."

"Oh, it's nothing," Quig said, grinning. "I learned it in lifesaving."

Their friends were in the water all around them, romping like a school of porpoises, celebrating the first day of summer vacation.

"Who wants to play baseball?" called Joe.

The boys were out of the river in an instant and racing off to the baseball diamond nearby. "Come on, Quig. Be bat boy."

"Not today," Quig decided. "I've got to take this kid brother of mine home."

"I'll come with you," Peggy said. "Wait till I get my jacket and shoes."

"I'm not going home now," Tommy announced, squirming to get free of Quig's detaining hand. "I'm gonna watch the guys play ball."

"No you're not," Quig told him. "You're going to come and let Mother decide what to do with you. You had no business starting out to the raft. If I've got to take care of you, then you're not going to do stupid stuff like that."

He picked up his white cane and draped his towel around his shoulders.

" 'Bye Quig," yelled Mike. "See you tomorrow after I've cut Johansons' grass."

The words hit Quig like a ten ton truck.

"O.K., see you," he agreed. He said it gaily enough, but inside he felt all let down. So Mike had

Johansons' yard to cut, too. That made four. And Joe and Don—all the guys had jobs. All but him. Why couldn't Mother and Dad see that he needed one, instead of just brushing off the idea every time he mentioned it. He'd decided against scout camp this summer just because he hoped to get one—well, that and the meet, too. But nobody seemed to think he had a chance.

"Come on," said Tommy. "Don't just stand there. I thought we were goin' home."

"O.K., O.K.," said Quig, bringing himself back to the problem at hand.

"Let's go along the river," he suggested to Peg.

It was his favorite walk. The narrow, grassy path beside the water was so much more interesting than the route through town. There were always birds and animals to hear in the thickets, and the little river made fascinating sounds on its way down to the mighty Mississippi. Quig stopped on a curve and stood listening for a moment. Peggy stopped and listened, too.

"What do you hear? I don't hear anything special," she said.

Quig started on down the path.

"No, I suppose you don't. I guess I wouldn't either if I could see," he said. "You look at the river and know that it's wide and quiet where we swim.

8

You can see that down here it gets narrow and very swift between the high bluffs. You see the rapids farther on, and then you see the falls. But I hear it instead of see it. That's why I always want to walk home this way."

"I never could hear those things," Peggy sighed.

"You could if you had to," Quig replied matter-of-factly. "Here's our turn. I suppose we'd better go home."

The Smiths and the Bradfords lived in the same block on Bluff Road, so Quig and Peg had grown up together. He hesitated wistfully on the path. This was his favorite place, this spot where their street came to a dead end at the high bluff above the river. There was a white wooden barricade that said, in big black letters, STOP—DEAD END. Beyond the sign was a wide, grassy place, and then the bank plunged sharply down to the water's edge. Stones formed a sort of crude natural stairway in the bluff. Tommy slithered up and down it like an otter, and Quig's friends fished in the swift water at the bottom; but the minute he, Quig, placed a foot on the first stone, someone always called out: "No point in getting your head bashed in, stupid!"

Quig's father had talked to him about it very seriously when he was little.

"You stay off Dead End, Quig," he had said with unusual sternness.

Quig had listened politely while his father went into detail about how dangerous Dead End Bluff was. With one part of his mind he was feeling afraid as he pictured the broken bones, the skinned nose and all the other damage he might suffer if he fell down the bluff. With the other part he was saying to himself, "Some day I'm going down Dead End. Some day I'm going." Yet he never had.

Many times his exploring foot had touched the first step, but there had always been someone to yell, "No, no, Quig!" or to snatch him back from the edge. He always wondered what would happen if no one called. Could he really make it; would he dare to if he had the chance? And what was equally to the point, should he? Would it be foolish even when it meant so much to him? Now that he was in junior high, in the summer before his ninth grade year, he was so busy that he hadn't brooded about the bluff as much as usual. This sunny afternoon, however, he felt again the longing to explore clear down to the rapids. He stood still on the grass, listening to the insistent whish of the water over the stones.

"Come on," Peggy urged impatiently. "What're you waiting for?"

Quig answered her, his voice suddenly harsh. "I'm going down Dead End some day, you know. It doesn't matter what any of you say. I've wanted to go, all my life!"

"Well, I won't hold my breath until you do," Peggy replied calmly. "This summer you'd better concentrate on beating the Valley boys in the free style. I'd rather you bashed your head in on the raft, if you must, than on the rocks at the bottom of Dead End Bluff."

"Thanks a lot!" said Quig. "We'd better go now. What's become of Tommy?"

"I'd like to think he's gone on home, but knowing your little brother, I doubt it," said Peggy. "He's vanished."

"Tom, where are you? Tommy!" Quig raised his voice in a shout that echoed up and down the bluff.

"Here I am," Tommy's voice drifted back on the breeze. "I'm going down to the Mississippi. Want to go along?"

"No!" Quig yelled back. "You come here or it'll be that much worse for you when you get home."

"Oh, all right," complained Tommy, and Quig could hear his feet stamping toward them along the path.

Chapter 2

Q**UIG WENT INTO THE HOUSE, TRAILING HIS CANE** in one hand and the reluctant Tommy in the other. They went past the silent living room, down the hall to the white colonial staircase. He could hear the sewing machine whirring in the back room where his mother always sewed, so he went up to find her.

"I guess I'll just go and get dressed now," suggested Tommy, as they passed his door.

"Uh-uh, we have business with Mother," Quig reminded him.

He pushed Tommy ahead of him into the sewing room.

"Well," she cried, stopping the machine. "Here

you are at last! I began to think you'd forgotten the way home. Been swimming all this time?"

"Not all the time," said Quig. "We came home by way of Dead End and had to wait for Tommy. He was heading out for the Mississippi."

"Oh, Tommy!" Quig heard the smile fade out of his mother's voice. "You know you never go there alone."

"I wasn't going alone," Tommy protested. "I was going there with Quig, only he wouldn't come."

"I certainly wouldn't!" Quig agreed. "Why should I go any place with him? What a dope! I was on the raft and he jumped into the deep water and started dog paddling out. It was lucky I got him."

"Yeah!" retorted Tommy, running over to stand in front of his mother, "He got me, all right. Talk about a dope! He dived in and swam under water and I didn't know where he was. He came up right under me and grabbed my feet. I might have drowned, that's what!"

"Oh, Quig!" his mother exclaimed. "You didn't pull him under, surely."

"I sure did," said Quig. "He's going to drown some day, anyway. He can't swim ten feet with that silly dog paddle, but he jumps in and takes off like a pro."

"Well, I've a feeling the best medicine for that is

13

a few days without any swimming," mused his mother.

"He can't go with me any more unless he behaves," Quig insisted. "If I'm going to practice for the meet, I can't spend all my time watching him."

"Now just a minute, Quig," his mother said firmly, "I'm sure he's a real nuisance to you when you swim, but that's one way you can help me in the summertime. I guess you're just going to have to keep your eye on him until he gets more sense."

Quig thought that over for a minute. "Well, O.K.," he said, "you mean keep my ear on him, don't you?" He went off to take his shower, still muttering a little to himself.

Later on, in his own room, he found a pair of freshly ironed brown shorts in the closet and picked a clean tan polo shirt out of the drawer. Long ago, when he first learned to read braille, his mother had devised a way for him to distinguish the color of his clothes. She had him braille the names of colors on his braillewriter, and then she cut them out and clipped them to his clothes each time she laundered them. Quig liked it because he didn't have to ask, but could go ahead with his dressing independently.

He had just finished dressing when he heard his father's car in the drive. His mother had gone down to the kitchen, and Quig heard her talking to him. He remembered then that they were having a picnic on the Mississippi shore with the Bradfords.

"Why don't you go down to the beach now and start the fire, Jeff?" Mother asked. "It takes so long to get good coals."

"Fine," Father agreed. "Wait till I change my clothes. I'm going for a swim after I get the fire started."

He and Quig met on the stairs. "Hi, want to go down to the beach with me and set things up?" he asked. "How's the water today?"

"Sure, I'll go. Water's getting warmer, but I'm not swimming tonight. Just got home from a long workout," Quig answered.

"O.K., Tommy and I'll swim," his father said, going on up the stairs.

"Tommy can't swim tonight," called Mother. "He got into trouble with Quig this afternoon and he's being punished. He tried to swim out to the raft after Quig told him to stay where it's shallow."

"The scamp!" Father said, with the little tinge of pride in his voice that Quig often detected when Tommy's exploits were being recited. "Glad he's got the spunk to try, anyhow. Time you and I taught him the real thing, Quig. He's been getting around with that dog paddle long enough."

"Do you think you could find that new bag of

charcoal for Dad?" his mother asked as he came into the kitchen.

Quig went out to the garage to look, brooding a little about his father's remark, remembering how often he had squelched his own "spunk to try!" In a way Quig felt sorry for his dad, though. It must have been quite a blow to have his first son born blind and not able to do a lot of the outdoor things he loved so well. And in all fairness, Quig had to admit that his father had taught him many of the things that had brought him so far along in scouting, all the things he hadn't learned at scout camp. He was a Life Scout now, well on his way to Eagle. It couldn't have been easy for his dad, watching him do so many potentially dangerous things. For some reason, maybe because he wasn't around as much, Dad had never been as easy about his exploring new things as Mother. Quig sighed and began the search for the charcoal. It was easy to see why it was fun for Dad to have Tommy.

Quig found the charcoal after picking up a wrong sack once or twice. Father met him at the back door; and they set out with Tommy, the thermos jug full of lemonade, and the hamburger patties. Mother and Mrs. Bradford would come along later with the rest of the food. Peggy came running out of her yard, three houses down the street.

"Dad's going to be a little late," she announced, joining the procession, "but he said to go on anyway, and he'll eat when he gets there. What a night for a picnic!"

"What a night to take the boat out, too," Quig added eagerly. "Can we?"

"After supper," his father agreed. "I want to swim now."

They walked along Bluff Road until they came to Dead End Bluff and turned left on the path along the river. Quig heard the water bubbling in the rapids, and he knew that soon it would spill over the low falls and rush out into the Mississippi. His feet followed the path expertly, because they came this way so often. His family owned a piece of land where the little river poured into the big one, and there his father had built a small boathouse just back of the sandy beach. They kept fishing rods and tackle and picnic paraphernalia in it, as well as boat equipment.

In a few minutes the grill was brought out, and father started the charcoal before he plunged into the river for his swim. Tommy watched wistfully from the shore.

"Want to fish, Peg?" Quig asked, getting his own fishing rod out and feeling cautiously in the tackle box for a plug. Last time he fished he had been a little hasty and caught a hook in his finger.

"Guess not tonight. I'm too lazy," said Peggy, lying back luxuriously in a beach chair.

Quig cast into the swift water at the mouth of the little river and reeled in slowly. He raised his arm backward to cast again when Peggy screamed, "Quig! Stop!"

Quig's arm froze halfway into another cast, and he heard a startled yelp.

"It's a dog," cried Peggy. "You've hooked him!"

Chapter 3

Q<small>UIG STOOD PERFECTLY STILL, AFRAID TO MOVE.</small>

"I can hear it's a dog," he yelled in exasperation. "Did I get his eye, or what? Where did he come from, anyway?"

"No, it isn't his eye. I don't know where he came from; never saw him before. He's got very thick fur, and your hook's caught in it somewhere."

Quig laid his rod down carefully and felt around for the dog.

"He's here, standing just as still," said Peggy. "There, boy—there. We'll have it out in a minute. Does it hurt?"

Quig knelt on the ground beside Peggy and found the dog with his hands. His fingers sank into the soft, deep coat, as he began searching gently for the hook.

"It's up near his head," Peggy directed. "I don't think it's caught in his skin. I think it's just in the fur. That fur's so thick it couldn't possibly get down to his hide."

"Good dog." Quig spoke soothingly to him. "If I didn't hook your hide, what made you yelp?"

"I think you just pulled his hair and it scared him," Peggy guessed. "Better let me; you can't see it."

She began to work at the hook, and the dog stirred uneasily and whimpered.

"Ooh! I'm hurting him," she said. "Maybe you'd better try after all, Quig."

She guided his hand to the spot, and his sensitive fingers found the hook almost immediately. Very carefully he began to work the point out of the incredibly thick fur.

Mr. Smith came dripping out of the river to investigate the commotion.

"What in the world? You certainly hooked a big one this time, Quig! Where did he come from? Never saw a dog like this around town."

"What kind is it?" Quig wanted to know. "I've never felt such a heavy coat."

"I don't know. He looks something like a husky and something like a German shepherd," Peggy

observed, "but his legs are too short. Feel his tail, Quig. It curls up over his back in a tight coil."

"I will in a minute," said Quig, continuing to disentangle the hook. "Hold still, boy. It's almost out. Now you're all right; it's loose!"

The dog gave him a grateful little whimper and a warm lick on his hand. Quig sat down beside him and ran his hands over the thick, springy coat, down to the curled tail, and up to the silky, perked ears.

A long shrill whistle sounded from up-river somewhere. He felt the dog's ears twitch in recognition. The whistle sounded again, closer now.

"Somebody's coming for him," Quig's father said.

Peggy threw her arms around the dog's furry neck. "You're a darling," she cried. "I wish we could keep you. I'll bet you're a cross between a husky and a shepherd."

Quig heard new steps on the beach. "Nope," a strange masculine voice answered. "He's not a crossbreed. You're looking at a thoroughbred Norwegian elkhound. This is Champion Storm of the Hollow."

Quig heard his father move toward the newcomer. "I'm Jefferson Smith," he introduced himself, "and these are my kids, Jefferson Quigley, junior, called Quig, and Tommy. This young lady is Peggy Bradford. We all live up on the Bluff Road."

"Well, then, I'm a neighbor," said the man. "We've just moved into the little green house up the river a bit, at the other end of Bluff Road. I'm George Munson."

"That's the old Adams' place. I heard it had been sold." Mr. Smith sounded pleased. "Do you have a family, Mr. Munson?"

"A boy and a girl, just about the size of your little guy, here," George Munson answered, "and my wife, Dorothy."

"You certainly have a wonderful dog," Quig

began eagerly. "I hooked him a minute ago, and he behaved like a gentleman while I was getting the hook out. I don't believe I hurt him. The hook just caught in his fur."

The man laughed. "I'm sure you didn't hurt him. It takes a lot to get through that coat. Storm's quite a dog. He's really the main reason we left the city and moved out here, as a matter of fact. Did he tell you he has a wife and children at home?"

"No," Quig said, entering into the spirit of the thing. "He only mentioned the hook in his fur."

"Sounds like him," continued Mr. Munson. "He couldn't care less about his family responsibilities. Six weeks ago Freya presented him with a litter of the most beautiful puppies you ever saw, and I doubt if he even remembers they're his. Come on, Storm. Let's go home. You can explore some more another day."

He snapped a leash on Storm's choke collar. Tommy ran over to pet the dog.

"Why did Storm make you move here?" he asked.

"Well, puppies make a lot of noise when they're little," explained Mr. Munson, "so we decided to move out where the neighbors wouldn't be so close."

"My goodness, are you going to keep them all?" cried Peggy in amazement.

"Oh no," Mr. Munson assured her. "We'll sell them as soon as they're old enough. They're pretty valuable pups. Storm already has his championship, and Freya is close to hers. Four of the pups are spoken for already by elkhound breeders."

"What's the rest of Freya's name? Does she have more, like Storm of the Hollow?" Quig asked.

"Yes, she's Freya of Pitch Road," said Mr. Munson. "Registered dogs are often named after their kennels. She was bred at the Pitch Road Kennels in Connecticut."

Quig knelt beside Storm again and ran his hand down the straight, sturdy back to the smoothly curled tail. It moved under his hand and Quig looked up at Mr. Munson delightedly.

"He's wagging it at me!"

Mr. Munson laughed. "Elkhounds aren't great tail-waggers, so when they do, you can take it as a real compliment."

Quig heard his mother's feet on the wooden steps that led down to the beach. Peggy's mother was with her, and they were carrying baskets of food.

"Stay and have some coffee and a hamburger with us," urged Mrs. Smith, after she had been introduced to Mr. Munson.

"Sorry," he said. "Got to get home and help my wife settle in. Thanks though. Any other time I'd love it. Come over soon and meet Dorothy and the youngsters. Quig, you come and get acquainted with the pups, and bring Peggy along."

"I will!" Quig promised.

George Munson disappeared up the shore with Storm of the Hollow, and Quig went into the boathouse to bring out the folding table for his mother. He set it up, and she and Mrs. Bradford began to lay out the food. His father had pulled on a shirt and was tending the meat on the grill.

"Bring some plates, Peg," he called. "They're done."

He tucked a hamburg patty into a bun for Quig. Mrs. Bradford helped him with ketchup and relish. His mother loaded his plate generously with the rest of the food, placing it in clock formation so he could know where each kind was.

"Your potato salad is at 12:00, baked beans at 12:15, and potato chips at 12:30," she briefed him.

He sat down on a log beside Peggy and applied himself silently to his food for several minutes. Finally he slowed down enough to talk.

"I certainly swam up a good appetite this afternoon!"

"I did, too," mumbled Peggy, her mouth full.

"I suppose you raced to the raft," remarked Quig's father. "Who won? This mermaid here?"

"Yes," Quig assured him. "I got off course and

missed the raft again. They told me I really beat her this time, but I lose the raft at the last minute every race."

"He's afraid of hitting his head," Peggy commented briefly. "He's got to get over it before the Midsummer Meet."

Everyone was silent for a few minutes. Quig thought the river must be looking-glass smooth because there was no sound from the water except the splash of a fish jumping far out in the channel. Then his father moved and cleared his throat.

"I wouldn't be too concerned about that if I were you, Quig," he said, trying to be casual, but Quig heard the tightness in his voice. "When you're racing, you come up to the raft with a lot of speed and force. You could really hit your head an awful wallop. Seems to me they could make some allowance for you. I know you don't like to ask, but after all, this is something special."

"I usually agree with you about being independent, Quig," his mother reminded him, "but I believe your father has a point here. If you go beyond the raft before the others get there, why haven't you won? I don't quite get it."

"No," said Quig firmly, "it wouldn't work at all. You see, this is a hundred yard race. It's only a hundred feet to the raft. We have to swim out and back and out again to make it. And if I keep overshooting the raft every time, I'll add an awful lot of mileage before the race is over!"

Peg's father had arrived and now joined the discussion. "Why don't they rig up a pole on the edge of the raft and let you touch that if you miss?" he wanted to know.

"No!" Quig answered decisively. "I'll do it right or I won't do it at all."

He moved impatiently and spilled lemonade all over his clean shirt. He dabbed at it awkwardly with his napkin.

Unexpectedly Peggy took his part. "You're right," she nodded. "You're such a good swimmer, I'll bet you make the team in high school. But if you do, you'll have to go by the rules that everybody else does. It wouldn't be fair to you to give you favors now."

"Well, you've got almost two months to do it in," his mother reminded him practically. "Jeff, if you're going to take the boat out, hadn't you better do it now? Seems to me it's getting a little cool."

Quig's father looked at his watch. "Eight o'clock already!" he exclaimed, jumping up. "Come on, kids, let's go. Quig, you get the cushions. Bill, d'you want to come along?"

Mr. Bradford swallowed his last bite of hamburger and helped get the boat ready for the water. *River Girl's* twenty-five horse motor purred

smoothly as Peg and Tommy and Quig climbed aboard. Peg's father pushed off from the little dock, and Mr. Smith headed upstream.

"The water is as smooth as satin," cried Peggy, "and it's streaked with silver and pink. O-o-oh, what a night to be on the river!"

Quig felt a familiar twinge of regret because he couldn't see the beauty that Peg did. But it didn't last because tonight he had something else on his mind. Something he had always wanted to do.

"Couldn't I run the motor, Dad, if you told me exactly what to do?" he begged. "I row, and I paddle the canoe all the time."

"That's different, Quig," his father answered. "This motor moves in a hurry. I don't think it would work."

"Have you ever thought of letting Quig handle the throttle while you steer, Jeff?" Peggy's father inquired. "That ought to be safe enough."

Mr. Smith cleared his throat in a meditative way. That meant he was thinking it over, Quig knew.

"All right, let's try it," he finally agreed.

He slowed the motor, and Quig felt *River Girl* turn toward shore.

"Shallow enough to change in here," said his father. "Move carefully."

Quig's heart was thudding with excitement as he crouched low in the boat and crawled past Mr.

Bradford onto the seat beside his father. He had
wanted to do this ever since he could remember.
His fingers found the motor controls, and he sat
tensely waiting. After brief directions, he set the
boat in motion, and his father steered out into the
river again. It was a temptation to open the throttle
wide and send the boat hurtling into the silky-
smooth current, but Quig used his judgment and
kept them moving along at a sober pace. He knew
that any future he might have with *River Girl*
depended upon this first trip.

He heard the throb of a dignified inboard on
their right. "Harrigans' cruiser?" he asked.

"Yes," marveled Peggy. "How did you know?"

"Oh, I could tell by the sound," Quig said. "There's a special little clunk, clunk to it."

"You can go a little faster," his father suggested. "Nothing ahead for quite a ways."

Quig pressed down on the lever gently, and *River Girl* leaped ahead. A dog barked suddenly on the bank and Peggy called, "Slow up, Quig. That's Storm and Mr. Munson. We're right opposite their house. Wave to them."

"Hi, Mr. Munson," shouted Tommy, waving madly. Peggy, who was sitting beside him in the stern, grabbed the back of his shorts to keep him from tumbling into the river.

Mr. Munson waved back, and Storm barked wildly. In a moment Quig heard a different bark echoing across the water. This one was higher and lighter in tone.

"That could be Freya," he guessed, letting *River Girl* idle in the sunset.

"Where?" demanded Peggy, forgetting that he couldn't see. "I just see Storm. Oh, there is another dog coming down to the dock. It's an elkhound. Sure, it must be Freya."

"Why don't you dock and come up?" called George Munson. "Freya wants to get acquainted."

"Couldn't we?" pleaded Quig and Peggy in unison.

"Let's go!" insisted Tommy.

30

"Not tonight. It's getting dark," said Quig's father. "Thanks, George. We'll come in the daytime. Haven't got any lights on the boat yet. Let's turn, Quig."

They circled in the quiet silver water and started back down-river. Quig could tell when they were nearing their own dock because the smell of hamburgers and burning charcoal and coffee still lingered on the air and came drifting out to them.

"Cut the motor," his father directed, and they glided in toward shore.

Quig could hear the women talking. It was his mother who saw them first.

"Ginny, look! Quig's running the boat!" This was followed by the sound of her feet hurrying out onto the dock.

"Quig, Daddy let you!" she exclaimed.

"It was Mr. Bradford's idea," Quig explained.

"There wasn't much on the river tonight," Mr. Smith said, as if to excuse himself. "Bill thought he could manage the speed if I steered, and he certainly did well. We'll give him another try some day."

He gave Quig a brisk pat on the back and snapped *River Girl's* rope to the ring on the dock. Coffee was keeping warm over the dying coals in the grill, and the grownups sat down for another cup, while Tommy and Quig and Peggy had more lemonade. The mothers produced sweaters, and they all sat on, reluctant to go home. They could hear the sleepy sound of birds in the bushes on the cliff, and far off across the river the call of a water bird.

"There's the first star," cried Tommy, breaking the quiet. "Starlight, star bright, first star I've seen tonight—what's the rest of it?"

"Wish I may, wish I might, have the wish I wish tonight," Quig finished.

"What do you wish tonight?" Peggy asked. "No, don't tell or you won't get it."

Quig laughed. "I'm not superstitious, so I guess it won't hurt if I tell. My wish would be to have one of the Munsons' puppies. And to have a job." He added the last rather defiantly. He knew what his parents felt on that subject. There was a moment's silence.

Then Peggy said, "I didn't know you were so crazy about dogs. Since when?"

"He's always loved dogs," Mrs. Smith said, "but I've discouraged his having one until he was old enough to take care of it himself. Maybe this is the time."

"Well, I like Storm better than any dog I've ever seen," Quig said emphatically.

"We'll have to see," his mother answered. "I've a feeling these puppies are pretty expensive."

"I s'pose they are," Quig agreed, "but let's go see

'em tomorrow, anyhow, Peg."

"O.K., I'll come down in the morning," she said, shivering a little in the evening air. "I'm getting cold."

"Let's go up," suggested her mother. "It's chilly as soon as the sun is gone."

The men doused the remaining coals in a bucket of water from the river and put the grill in the boathouse. Everybody gathered up the rest of the picnic things and straggled up the long flight of steps to the top of the cliff. Peggy stumbled in the dark and Quig grabbed her arm.

"Careful," he warned her. "Better hang onto me."

They walked back along the path high above the Mississippi to Dead End Bluff. Tommy ran on ahead with his mother and Mrs. Bradford. The men were talking business in the middle, and Peggy and Quig brought up the rear. They stopped a moment when they reached the bluff.

A bullfrog croaked hoarsely in the darkness, and a little peeper frog replied in gentle treble.

Peggy pulled at Quig's arm. "Let's go home," she urged, with a little shudder. "I think the Dead End is scary and mysterious at night, don't you?"

"I never thought much about it," replied Quig shortly. "It's the same to me at night as it is in the daytime; but come on, let's go home."

Chapter 4

QUIG AWAKENED THE NEXT MORNING AND LISTENED
for sounds in the house. He stretched and yawned
luxuriously. Perfect heaven to have school out and
the long, wonderful summer ahead! He could lie
in bed as long as he pleased, and Dad wouldn't come
in to hustle him out for the long ride into town.
Ever since first grade Quig had been riding into the
city each morning with his father, so that he could
go to school with several other blind children.

He had been enrolled in a regular classroom with
sighted children, but there was a resource room in
the school where he went for part of the day with
the others who couldn't see. There he learned to
write on his brailler, to read braille swiftly with his

fingers, and to type on an ordinary typewriter.

He had learned "mobility" there, too—how to get around comfortably in the school and at home, practicing "trailing," with his right hand flung out to guide him along the wall, and his left arm across his chest in a protective position, to keep him from injury. He had been taught many other devices that made it possible for him to get along a good deal like other children who could see with their eyes.

It had been in this same school, near the end of his sixth grade year, that his resource teacher had said to him, one day, "Quig, I've been watching you very carefully lately, and I think you're ready to learn cane travel. Am I right?"

He was ready all right. He could hardly wait. So a teacher who was an expert in this had come to teach him to use the white cane. After that, with much more freedom, many of the dead ends had disappeared.

By the end of his seventh grade year, however, he had begun to feel discontented in another way. He liked the itinerant teacher who came several times a week to help him, and everyone at school was friendly, but somehow he just didn't seem to belong there.

Since learning cane travel, he went everywhere in Scott by himself. He swam and fished with his friends all summer. He practically managed the baseball team, and when there was a picnic he took his guitar along so they could sing. He belonged to Boy Scouts in his church, and went to camp with them. Nobody paid much attention to his blindness, and he was one of the most popular boys in the neighborhood, but when fall came and school started again, it was a different story. Peggy and Joe and Don and Mike and all the others went off to Jackson School together, while he went into the city every morning. They tried to include him in their plans just as they did in the summertime, but it wasn't the same.

Now, reveling in laziness, Quig let his mind stray past the summer just beginning. In the fall he was going to stay at home and go to ninth grade with his friends, with an itinerant teacher coming out several days a week to give him extra help. He would go to all the games and the parties, and do everything everyone else did. He might even get on the swimming team some time. Just thinking about it was tremendously exciting. He jumped out of bed and began to dress in a rush.

He opened the case of his braille watch and felt for the time. It was after 8:30. He could hear Tommy yelling in the back yard. Dad must already have gone to the office. The sun was shining, and it was going to be a glorious day—a patch of floor felt warm to his bare feet as he crossed it on his way to the open window. The breeze that came in was mild, too, and it carried the smell of warm earth and early flowers in the garden. Now if he could only get a job, everything would be perfect.

He went downstairs and needed nothing but the smell of frying bacon to hurry him to the kitchen. He could hear it sputter as Mother turned it in the skillet.

"I'm at the stove," she said, breaking an egg into the hot grease.

Her habit of locating herself had always saved him from that uncomfortable feeling of being in the presence of someone without being sure. Now he walked confidently over and slid into his chair at the breakfast table. He found his napkin and put it in his lap. Mother turned the egg and he could hear the gentle, soft plop that it made in the pan.

"It's another lovely day," she remarked. "Your orange juice is in front of you."

Quig drank it and smacked his lips with pleasure. "Mmm, good. Feels as though it's going to be a good swimming day. Don't give me my egg until I get a piece of toast made."

He slipped a piece of bread into the toaster and sat back to wait. Mother put some bacon on his plate, and he picked it up in his fingers and nibbled while the toaster put-putted along. It popped up, and Mother brought the egg and put it on the hot toast. She sat down to talk while he ate.

"How do you really feel about the Midsummer Meet, Quig? Do you really want to enter it, or is everybody pushing you into it?"

"Gee, I don't know," he answered, pushing his plate over for her to cut the toast. "May I have some more milk, please? I want to swim the free style, but I certainly don't want to make an idiot of myself. Do you think Peg's right? Am I scared of hurting myself? I've never been before that I can remember."

"I don't know." Mother was matter-of-fact in her response. She poured him a glass of milk and moved over to the sink to wash dishes. "Peg's pretty smart, and she's seen you swim a lot more than I have. It could be."

"I've a feeling Dad isn't too keen about my entering."

Quig groped for a piece of egg that had slipped off onto the table. There was a long pause while Mother ran hot water over the greasy plates.

"Quig, you're old enough now to begin to understand your father," she said slowly. "He's scared to death to have you do anything where you might be hurt. He's fought against the feeling all your life, but if he'd had his way he would have wrapped you in cotton wool and kept you under glass."

She laughed, but Quig thought there wasn't

much humor in the sound.

"Why is he that way?" he demanded. "It must have been twice as hard for you, and it's been tough for me, all right."

His mother sighed and put the silver into the drainer. "It has been hard. Sometimes I feel as though I've had to battle every inch of the way for your freedom. But when I stop to think why he feels that way, Quig, I can be patient. It's because he loves you so terribly much that he's afraid for you. Can you understand that?"

"Oh, I know," Quig assured her. "But I can't see what made him that way. You would think a mother would be much—well, you know, scarier."

Mother wiped the silver and put it in the drawer and laughed—really laughed this time. "Maybe I would have been 'scarier,' Quig, if I hadn't been with you all the time. I could see, as soon as you began to crawl, that you'd have to be allowed to do things if you were going to grow up to be a normal man. You were a super-adventuresome, exploratory baby. It wasn't easy to turn you loose, I can tell you!"

"Yeah, I s'pose," Quig nodded. "But now, to get back to the swimming meet—do I enter it?"

"Why, of course!" Quig heard the strong confidence that had always "turned him loose." "Work at it just as hard as you can all summer and by the end of July you'll go in there and hit the raft, and I don't mean with your head, either."

They both laughed, and Quig heard Peg at the back door.

"What's so funny?" she wanted to know.

She came into the kitchen, and Quig explained.

"Great!" she cried. "We'll practice every day, and you'll be finding the raft in no time; but I don't want to go until this afternoon. The water's so cold in the mornings. Brrrr! Let's go to see the puppies now."

Tommy came running in to show them a frog he had caught.

"I want to go see the puppies, too," he announced, dropping the frog on the table.

"Ooooh!" screamed Peggy. "Take that horrible thing away! We'll all get warts."

"Warts?" Quig roared with laughter. "Who ever heard of warts from a frog? It's an exploded theory, even with toads. Get it out of here, though, Tom. Does he have to go to the Munsons' with us, Mom? Don't you think it would be better for us to go alone the first time?"

Tommy set up an indignant howl.

"I don't think it will hurt you any to take him," his mother said firmly. "After all, they do have children his age. Here, Tommy, put your frog in this jar and punch some holes in the lid."

The frog leaped off the table and Tommy chased it around the room. Peggy accepted a hot piece of toast from Mrs. Smith and drew her feet up under her. "D'you s'pose we ought to call Mrs. Munson first?" she asked. "We've never met her."

"Why?" Quig inquired. "They probably haven't even got a phone in yet. Let's just walk over and introduce ourselves. Mr. Munson said to come. And on the way I want to stop around by the drugstore and see if I can get that job. Mr. Wilson's got a 'boy wanted' sign in the window, Mike told me."

Quig could feel the silence that descended upon the room. His mother stood still at the sink, and Peggy stopped chewing her toast. They seemed to be waiting each other out. It finally fell to Peggy to begin. He heard an uncomfortable little sigh before she spoke.

"I wouldn't bother," she said. "All the younger kids were waiting at the door practically at dawn. Mike said his brother went down. This is a job even twelve-year-olds can do. There isn't much they can find to do in the summertime."

"Yeah," Quig said rather bitterly, "and there isn't much I can find to do, either. I'm going anyhow. Maybe he'd rather have an older boy if he could get one, and there're lots of things I could do in a store if somebody'd give me a chance."

Quig heard his mother clear her throat as though

to speak, but it was Peggy who continued.

"Sure there are," she agreed, "but not this job, Quig. Mr. Wilson wants a boy to deliver on his bike."

"Oh," said Quig, and all the anticipation went out of his face. "No, I guess you're right. I couldn't do that."

Now his mother took up the conversation. "Don't you worry about a job, Quig. Your father and I have been thinking of more things that need doing around here this summer, things that you can do very well. Dad will pay you for doing them, of course."

Quig got up and walked toward the door. Because he was disappointed and upset, he wasn't as careful as usual, and fell over a chair. He picked himself up and said impatiently, rubbing his shin, "Mother, can't you understand that this isn't the kind of job I want? I'm tired of puttering around with all the piddling little jobs you and Dad lie awake nights dreaming up for me. Summer's a lot of fun, but I get awful sick of not having a real job when all the rest of the guys do. Come on, Peg. Let's go down to see the pups. If Mike comes from his job before I'm back, Mom, tell him to wait."

His mother said nothing, but as he slammed out the door, Quig could feel the distress he left behind him in the kitchen.

Chapter 5

It was a beautiful morning to be outdoors. Quig and Peggy walked down Bluff Road, with Tommy running on ahead as usual. The road twisted and turned through gently rolling green lawns and bright gardens, tall old trees and pleasant houses. They passed the house where Don lived; but he was nowhere to be seen, and they decided not to stop. As Peggy said, probably it would be better not to take the whole neighborhood to see the puppies first thing.

After a few blocks Bluff Road angled toward the Mississippi and unexpectedly they were there. At the end of the road a low, green-shingled house sat in back of a white picket fence. The back yard sloped down to the river and the dock where they had seen Mr. Munson the night before. Just as Peggy reached out to open the gate, a pair of children came racing around the house.

"Hey, Mom, we've got company," the little girl called back over her shoulder.

In a moment a young woman appeared, lugging a big packing box.

"Goodness," Peggy whispered to Quig, "She doesn't look much older than I do."

She set the box down and pushed the hair back out of her eyes. "I'm Mrs. Munson," she said cordially. "Do come in and get acquainted. We're still unpacking. I've been looking everywhere for this box of kitchen things, and just found it in the garage, of all places!"

Quig listened very carefully as they accepted her invitation to come in. He liked Mrs. Munson immediately. Her voice was alive and glowing. He didn't need to see her smile; he could hear it flowing through her voice. Peggy would tell him later whether she was pretty or not, what kind of clothes she wore, and many other little details, but he already knew what he needed to know.

"Oh, so you're Quig," she said. "My husband told me that you went fishing and caught Storm last night!"

There was none of the "oh, you poor boy, so

you're blind" sound to her words. He felt sure that she knew he was blind, but evidently she didn't propose to make anything of it. Quig relaxed.

Tommy went off to play with the children, Peter and Marcella. Mrs. Munson excused herself for a few minutes; and when she came out of the house, Quig heard the tinkle of ice in a pitcher and glasses on a tray.

"I've been working since dawn," she said, "and I'm just done in. Let's have some lemonade."

She poured a glass for everyone and passed a plate of "store" cookies. Suddenly Quig heard another noise—a whimper of greeting, and Storm came tearing across the lawn to them. He flung himself upon Quig, and lemonade cascaded everywhere.

"My goodness!" exclaimed Dorothy Munson, "My husband said Storm liked you, Quig, but I had no idea it was love at first sight."

"I wondered where he was," Quig replied, hugging Storm delightedly.

"I had him shut in the house, the rascal," Mrs. Munson explained. "I didn't want him running off down the river again. This time I would have had to chase him myself."

"Why didn't he bark when he heard us out here?" Peggy wondered. "I thought dogs always barked when people came to their houses."

"Not Storm," Mrs. Munson answered, replenishing Quig's lemonade, "although he barked a lot when he was a puppy. Since he's grown up, he's learned that gentlemen dogs don't bark unless the newcomer isn't welcome. He always whimpers to greet the family and friends. Hearing me talking to you in a friendly way, he wouldn't bark at you, but usually he has to know someone quite a while before he whimpers. That's why I was so surprised when he whimpered at you, Quig. He's really lost his heart in a hurry."

"Me, too!" Quig exclaimed. "He seems so gentle. Isn't he ever cross with strangers?"

"Oh, yes," Mrs. Munson said, reaching out to pet him. "He shakes the rafters when he thinks a stranger doesn't belong, and somehow he always seems to know. The hair on the back of his neck bristles, and he really looks quite vicious. More lemonade, anybody?"

"No, thank you," said Peggy, politely. "It was nice of you to fix it for us when you're so busy."

Mrs. Munson laughed. "This little visit has been a lifesaver for me. Shall we go and see Freya and the puppies now?"

Quig jumped up. "Could we, please?" he asked. "Where are they?"

"They're in the shed," Mrs. Munson said, leading the way across the back yard. "That's one reason we chose this place. The little shed makes a perfect kennel. Mr. Munson's going to fence in a run for them soon. I have to keep Freya shut up when he isn't home. It's time to wean the puppies, and she's bored to death with the whole business. If I let her out, she might be off for a half day's jaunt. Come on, Storm, you stay with us."

Mrs. Munson unfastened the door of the shed and stood back for the others to go in. Quig heard a gentle welcoming sound as Freya saw her mistress, and then a tumult of excited puppy yaps.

"They're here against the wall to your left, Quig," Mrs. Munson directed, much as his mother would have. "You sit down on the floor beside the box, and I'll put some of them out for you to play with."

Quig squatted down on the straw-covered floor and waited. Freya jumped out of the box and brushed against him. "Will she care if we handle them?" he wanted to know.

"Oh, no," Mrs. Munson assured him, "not if you're gentle. I never let too many people in to see the puppies at one time."

She reached into the box. "Here, Quig," she said, and laid a fat, warm puppy in his arms. "And here's one for you, Peggy."

Peggy spilled a torrent of excited baby-talk into the puppy's ear.

Quig simply sat still and felt the one he held very carefully all over. Suddenly he said, "Now I know what he looks like. He's exactly like the teddybear I used to have. What's his name, or haven't they been named yet?"

"Yes," answered Mrs. Munson. "They're all registered, and naturally they have to be named first. The one you have is the image of his father. We have pictures of Storm when he was a puppy and you couldn't tell them apart, so we called him Viking Storm of the Hollow, and your baby, Peggy, has a real Norwegian name. She's called Freya's Signe."

Freya went over to Quig and sniffed of him. Then she licked his hand, as if to say, "You're all right." Viking wriggled to get down, so Quig reluctantly let him go and reached out to play with the others. The puppies romped and rolled and squealed in their play until they were tired and it was time to put them back into the box. Suddenly Quig felt something warm and furry climb into his lap again. He smoothed it with his sensitive hands and said tentatively, "It's Viking, isn't it?"

"It is indeed," marveled Mrs. Munson. "Like father, like son. He loves you, Quig."

"I certainly would like to buy him," Quig announced unexpectedly.

"Oh!" exclaimed Mrs. Munson. Quig detected a

startled note in her voice.

"What's the matter?" he asked in alarm. "Is he one of the four that's already spoken for?"

"No, he isn't," said Mrs. Munson slowly. "But only because he's so expensive. We are asking a pretty high price for Viking because he's the best of the litter. I told you, remember, that he is exactly like his father, and Storm is a rather famous champion, for such a young dog."

Quig felt as though someone had thrown cold water over him, but he persisted. "What do you mean by 'a pretty high price' for a dog? Do you mean twenty-five or thirty dollars, or maybe fifty? I have twenty-five in the bank and I think I might get five dollars more for my birthday."

Mrs. Munson hesitated for such a long time that Quig thought she hadn't heard him. "Would thirty be enough?" he ventured.

"I'm afraid it wouldn't be, Quig," she finally answered with regret in her voice. "You see, Storm and Freya each come from a long line of elkhounds with very excellent pedigrees. They are splendid show dogs, and their puppies will be, too. We expect some breeder to buy Viking Storm for around two hundred dollars."

"Two hundred dollars!" gasped Quig. Then he fell silent while they walked out of the shed. How he needed a job! At last he said resolutely, "My twenty-five will be a starter. I can earn more."

Tommy and Marcy and Pete came dashing up the steps from the beach.

"Look what Pete found for me!" Tommy yelled, running up to Quig. "He caught these frogs in his minnow net. Here, Quig, hold 'em while I go see the puppies."

He thrust two wriggling green frogs into Quig's hands and raced off into the shed after the other children.

"Oh, oh!" said Quig, as one of the frogs leaped out of his hands into the grass. "Come on—help me catch him, Peg."

He squatted down and began to fumble in the grass with his free hand.

"I will not!" Peggy refused. "Anything but that!"

Mrs. Munson giggled. "Don't lose the other one. I'll get a box."

She ran into the garage and came back with a small carton. Quig held the other frog while she clapped the box upside down over the fugitive. In a minute the crisis was over and both frogs were secure in the box.

"Hurry up, Tommy. Let's go home," Quig called.

Chapter 6

THE WHOLE CROWD WENT SWIMMING THAT AFTER-
noon. Even Joy and Liz, who hated cold water,
turned up. The small river still held a memory of
the Minnesota winter, but nobody cared because
the sun was so warm. Quig practiced the free style
over and over again, back and forth from the beach
to the raft, not even trying to touch it—just working to improve his speed. Joe was working on the
backstroke, Don practiced the butterfly, and the
girls took diving instruction from Mike, who was
the champion in that department.

A little while before it was time to go home,
Peggy stopped diving and raced with Quig. This
time he made the raft, directed by the shouts of his

friends, but slowed up noticeably at the last minute, so Peggy beat him by a length.

Mike was the authority on the Green Valley swimmers; he went down to scout them from time to time.

"You've gotta swim full speed right up to the last, Quig," he insisted, "or you'll never beat Chuck Hanson. He's sure fast."

"O.K." agreed Quig. "Have you got enough wind to try it again, Peg?"

They plunged in once more and churned their way back and forth. This time he swam furiously and came up far ahead of Peggy, but veered off at the moment of victory and shot beyond the raft. He paddled back and pulled himself up beside the others with a groan of disgust.

"Never mind," Liz said. "You'll get the combination before the meet. Chuck Hanson'll have to go some to beat you! You're going to bring the trophy back to Scott."

"Thanks," Quig said grimly, "but I won't believe it until I get that combination."

"Three of us will have to enter the free style; there have to be three," pondered Mike. "I think I'd better, although I'm not much good. I'll be diving, so that won't take as much wind as the other swimming events. Peggy can be the third one. She'll probably peter out, but she's good while she lasts."

53

Quig stayed with the boys for a while when they went to play baseball, but he felt so discouraged that he wandered off to be alone at his favorite spot on Dead End Bluff.

Tommy came along later and found him sitting there, brooding over his swimming problem.

"Go on home, Tommy," Quig ordered abruptly. "I don't feel like having you around this afternoon."

"I am not going home," retorted Tommy. "I just got here. I'm going down Dead End to look for that big old bullfrog we heard the other night when we had our picnic."

He climbed over the white barricade and started down the bluff, his tin can rattling against the stones. Soon Quig heard him splashing around in the shallow water, slipping on the rocks.

"Don't fall into the rapids," he called down.

"Who's gonna fall?" Tommy called back smartly. "I been down here three times today, looking for that old frog."

In a little while he came scrambling back up the bluff. "Gee, it's fun down there," he said, "but why d'you s'pose I can't find that frog?"

"I don't know," replied Quig. "Maybe he only comes out at night. What're you going to do with him if you do catch him? They're huge, you know. He'd probably eat all the others up."

"You know I'm making a collection," Tommy explained. "I got two toads now, and three little frogs, but I want that big old frog. He would not eat 'em up."

"Well, let's go home now," Quig suggested. "Maybe you better look for him at night. But I wouldn't worry about it, you've got all summer."

That evening the whole Smith family walked down to the Munsons to invite them for a beach supper on Saturday. Storm and Freya greeted them heartily, and while everyone else in the family looked at the puppies, Mr. Munson took Quig aside for a talk.

"Do you have a job lined up for the summer, Quig?" he began.

"Why no, I don't," answered Quig in surprise.

He felt warm all over. Mr. Munson just seemed to take it for granted that he would eventually have a job. Maybe he didn't know how hard it was to find a summer job if you weren't quite fourteen, and blind.

"My wife told me how well you got along with the dogs today," Mr. Munson went on, "and I've been wondering if I could get you to help out with the pups. Freya's starting to wean them now, and that means they will be a terrific care for Mrs. Munson. What with the house to settle and the kids to look after, I'm afraid she's going to have a pretty rugged summer. When the puppies are weaned, they have to be fed five times a day for a while, and that's going to tie her down."

Quig couldn't believe his ears. He could scarcely frame an answer. Mr. Munson was asking *him* to "help out with the pups!" A job had come to *him*. And what a job!

"I'm sure I could," he managed to reply. "I certainly would like to!"

Mr. Munson continued. "My idea was that you could come over at least once a day and help with feeding until you got used to it. Then if Mrs. Munson wanted to go away for an afternoon, say, you could take over. Could you give that much time to it? Of course, you'd be paid."

Quig flushed. He wanted more than anything in

the world to be paid so that he could save money to buy a puppy—the puppy— but imagine being paid to do something he'd love so much!

He hesitated just a second and then said decidedly, "I wouldn't need to be paid for it, Mr. Munson. Gee, it'd be enough just to be around the dogs every day."

Mr. Munson was equally decided. "No, Quig. This is a business proposition. We will agree on a fair amount. Saturdays and Sundays I'll be at home, so usually you wouldn't need to come then. Some days you would come only once, but other days you might come several times and stay for fairly long periods, if Mrs. Munson should be away. Does five dollars a week seem reasonable to you?"

It seemed wonderful. Mr. Munson reached for Quig's hand, and they sealed the bargain with a firm shake. It only remained to tell the family and receive final permission.

Quig detected the familiar tightness in Dad's voice as he spoke.

"George, do you think he can do it satisfactorily? It seems like quite a responsibility for a boy his age."

Quig knew what was in his father's mind and he waited, scarcely breathing, for the answer.

"We won't ask him to do it alone until he's had plenty of practice, Jeff," George Munson assured him. "I'm sure it will work out fine. Dorothy says he's a natural with dogs, and I saw myself how Storm took to him last night."

"I think he can do it all right, Jeff," Quig's mother said quickly. "He's always been so responsible with Tommy. Goodness, he's taken care of him ever since he was a puppy!"

Quig's embarrassment at all the attention was lost in the laugh that followed his mother's remark. Mrs. Munson made iced tea and a pitcher of lemonade, and they were all having some, sitting on the grass in the warm June twilight, when Quig heard a car stop in the road. The door slammed and the footsteps of a man and a woman came toward them. Mr. Munson walked to the gate to meet them. Storm, lying beside Quig, leaped to his feet and began to bark furiously.

"Good evening, can I be of help?" George Munson asked.

"I think you can," a pleasant masculine voice replied. "I'm Henry Whitford and this is Mrs. Whitford. We're quite interested in buying an elkhound puppy, and I was told by a friend of yours that you have a splendid litter on hand. I wondered if we could see them."

"Why, of course," answered Mr. Munson. "We're always glad to show the dogs. As a matter of fact, we're pretty proud of this litter. Who told you about us?"

"Allen Nelson," Mr. Whitford told him. "We'd been directed to him by the Kennel Club, but he doesn't have any pups for sale. He sent us to you. Said your dogs have excellent blood lines—better than his, actually."

George Munson laughed. "Well, that was very generous of Al," he said. "Come and look at the pups."

Storm had come back to his position beside Quig, but now he followed suspiciously at the visitors' heels as they went into the shed. In a few minutes they came out again and joined the group on the lawn.

"Oh, did you ever see such adorable puppies?" gushed Mrs. Whitford in a high-pitched voice that Quig found oddly unpleasant. "And this is their daddy, isn't it?"

She reached down to pet Storm's smooth head. He growled deep in his throat. Quig could feel the vibration as the dog drew back and pressed against his side.

"You mustn't be afraid of me," coaxed Mrs. Whitford, leaning toward Storm. "I love pretty dogs like you!"

He isn't afraid of you; he just doesn't like you, thought Quig to himself, detecting again the sweet heaviness of the perfume she wore. He had noticed it immediately when she first came into the yard. Now his supersensitive nose wrinkled involuntarily in dislike.

Mr. Munson spoke a quieting word to Storm. He stopped growling and let Mrs. Whitford touch him, but he was tense against Quig's side. Mr. Whitford lit a pipe, and the mild fragrance of his tobacco curled up into the still air.

"Those are handsome pups," he began. "Now, let's get down to cases. You say four of them are spoken for already. I hope the top dog of the litter isn't one of them, because if he is, we can't do business. I want nothing but the best. We're thinking of breeding, and of course we'd want the best stock available. I'm prepared to pay a good price to get it, too."

"Of course," approved Mr. Munson. "Viking Storm is the best, and he's still available."

Quig stiffened. Viking—his puppy—the one he had marked for his own some day! He shivered in the warm evening.

"I'd like a look at his pedigree," the man was saying.

"Come into the house," Mr. Munson invited. "We've just moved in, but I guess you can get around the packing boxes."

Mrs. Whitford stayed with the people on the lawn.

60

"Where is your home?" Mrs. Munson asked.

"We've been living in Minneapolis," she replied, "but we're getting ready to move out to the west coast some place where it's warmer. I can't stand this cold climate."

After what seemed an endless time to Quig, the men came out of the house.

"Let's go dear," Mr. Whitford said to his wife. "You've never seen such a pedigree as these pups have! Maybe we ought to buy the whole litter."

He laughed and started his wife toward the car, Storm following close at their heels.

"Good night," he called. "I'll be getting in touch with you in a month or so when the pup is ready to go."

"Very good," Mr. Munson answered. "Meantime he'll have all his shots and be set."

The car door shut, the motor whirred, and the Whitfords were gone. Quig made a mental note, as he always did about cars, that this one was probably a late model Ford.

Mr. Munson was impressed with the Whitfords. "He's got the best of bank references," he said, "and he certainly was thorough. He copied down the pedigree, word for word. I believe he's really serious about breeding. Never turned a hair when I told him what we were asking for Viking."

A little later the Smiths said good night and

walked up Bluff Road in the dusk. Much of the joy had gone out of the new job for Quig. Viking would soon be gone forever, beyond his reach. Probably he could never have earned all that money, anyhow; but as long as the puppy was with the litter, there would still have been a chance.

They turned up their own walk, and down at the bottom of Dead End Bluff Tommy's big old bullfrog bellowed glumly in the dark.

Chapter 7

Q<small>UIG WALKED INTO</small> M<small>UNSONS</small>' <small>YARD ALONE ONE</small>
morning to take care of the puppies. It was a lovely
June day. A soft breeze blew in from the river, and
the wonderful smell of freshly cut grass was in the
air. Mrs. Munson had telephoned early to ask if he
could manage by himself this morning, because she
had to take the children to the dentist at nine. This
was his first chance to be alone with the dogs, and
he was whistling with satisfaction as he found the
path with his cane and headed toward the house.
Storm heard the whistle and whimpered a greeting,
then exploded into a riot of ecstatic barks.

"Coming, boy," Quig called, finding the key
under the mat and fumbling to open the back door.

Storm rushed at him, almost upsetting him in his excitement. Quig stopped to pet him for a minute and then went to the refrigerator for the puppies' food. He took the ground beef, in the familiar pan, to the stove for warming. Mrs. Munson had taught him to light the stove with the pilot light and tell by feeling the meat when it was warm enough. The milk had to be warmed a bit, too, so Quig did that while he waited for the meat. Storm danced around impatiently, whimpering his eagerness to go out to the shed with Quig.

The chill was off the meat in a few minutes, and Quig went out with it first. He had to very careful on the steps—capering dog, pan of food, long white cane. It would be an awful mess if he fell. He didn't. Freya and the puppies met him cordially, and he let Freya out into the run that Mr. Munson had built. Then he fed the puppies. Viking was always first at the pan, with Signe a close second. Quig could tell by feeling them that these two were the largest and sturdiest of the pups.

He went back to the house for their milk; and as he returned with the enameled pail in his hand, he heard a car stop at the gate. Someone got out and came into the yard. Storm, running at Quig's heels as he always did, left him and ran toward the visitor, barking with the hostile sound that Quig had come to recognize.

"If you were my dog, I'd teach you to quit that, you big brute!" Quig heard a high-pitched female voice exclaim, and then the swishing sound of a stick slashed through the air.

"Come, Storm!" Quig shouted.

Storm whirled back and pressed against his side, a ferocious growl vibrating in his throat. Quig held the dog's choke collar and walked toward the woman. He was almost certain who she was. Scarcely ever had he been wrong about a voice; and just then, as he approached her, a whiff of heavy-sweet perfume came to him on the June breeze, mingled with the fragrance of grass and roses. That was it. There was no question in his mind, now.

"You're Mrs. Whitford, aren't you?" he asked, hanging tightly to Storm's collar. "I'm Quig Smith. I take care of the puppies. Can I help you?"

"Yes," responded Mrs. Whitford, tartly. "Keep that dog off me."

Then her voice changed and took on the sticky sweet tone that Quig remembered. It seemed to go with her perfume.

"I can't think why he has taken such a dislike to me. Animals always love me. Is Mrs. Munson here?"

"No, she isn't," Quig answered in as pleasant a voice as he could muster. "She's away with the children this morning."

"Oh!" exclaimed Mrs. Whitford. "So she leaves you alone with the puppies. My goodness, does she do it very often? I should think it would be risky to trust all these valuable pups to a blind boy. What if something should happen? You couldn't do a thing."

Storm was still growling deep in his throat and Quig felt like joining him in a growl, too. Blind boy, indeed!

"They're perfectly safe with me. I've been well-trained for my job," he answered.

"Well, I want to see our dog," said the woman, irritation becoming noticeable in the whine. "I was driving by and just thought I'd drop in."

She followed Quig into the shed and watched while he poured the milk into the pans. The puppies swarmed over and began to lap thirstily.

"Which one is mine?" she asked. "I don't suppose you can tell them apart, though."

"Oh, yes, I can tell them apart, all right. At least I couldn't miss Viking and Signe," Quig assured her.

He knelt down beside the puppies and began to run his hands gently over them. Signe stopped drinking and licked his hand and Viking polished off the last drop and climbed up Quig's knee.

"Here he is," said Quig.

"Oh, isn't he cute!" gushed Mrs. Whitford. "Let me have him."

She snatched at the puppy by his fat little front legs, and he yelped in pain.

"Don't do that!" cried Quig. "You'll hurt him. Pick him up around his body, like this." And he picked Signe up to show her how.

"You can't tell me how to handle dogs," said Mrs. Whitford. "I was working with dogs long before you were born. He's been coddled too much. We'll soon train that out of him. I'm going to take him out on the lawn now and see how he runs."

She started toward the door with Viking in her arms, but Quig moved in front of it with Storm at his side to bar the way.

"No," he said firmly, "I can't let you do that. You see, he hasn't been trained to come when he's called yet, and he might run away. You're welcome to play with him in here."

"Well, I like that!" cried the woman furiously.

"I guess this is my dog, and I'll do as I please with him. Get out of my way."

"Excuse me," said Quig, feeling the hot, red blood surge up into his face, "but Viking is not your dog, yet. Until you pay for him, he's the Munsons' dog, and I'm responsible for him."

The woman took another step toward Quig, and Storm snarled and lunged at her. Quig grabbed for his collar and jerked him back. Mrs. Whitford dropped Viking hastily and jumped out of the way.

"All right," she said angrily, "if you're going to make a fuss about it, I'll go. But the Munsons will hear about this, never fear. I'll tell them how impertinent you were."

She stalked out of the shed, and a moment later Quig heard the car start and spatter gravel as it lunged away down the road toward town. He finished taking care of the dogs, with shaking hands, fastened them in with Freya again, put Storm in the kitchen and started for home. Mrs. Munson and the children should be home any minute, but he decided not to wait. With Freya to guard the puppies, they should be safe enough. He was seething with a mixture of anger and apprehension. Would Mr. Munson think he had been impudent, or what did that woman call it? Impertinent?

He ate his lunch with his mother on the cool back porch and told her about it. "Do you think I

68

was impertinent, Mother?" he finished.

Mrs. Smith hesitated for a minute before she answered, and then she said, "Well, Quig, I don't think the words you said were impertinent. It depends entirely upon how you said them. Did you say them impudently?"

Quig flushed. "I don't know, Mom," he answered. "Maybe it sounded sassy. I was just telling her. Honestly, I was so mad, and I still am!"

That evening Quig went down to Munsons' to help with the feeding and tell about his experience with Mrs. Whitford. Mr. Munson listened in silence except for little mumbling sounds of sympathy and approval once in a while. At the end Quig said, "Gee, Mr. Munson, I'm sorry if I queered your sale or anything, but I didn't think you'd want Viking running around loose in the yard. We never could have gotten him if he'd taken it into his head to run off, and besides, he could have run out into the road."

"You were absolutely right, Quig," George Munson assured him. "I'd rather not make the sale than have anything happen to Viking. Maybe I ought to do some further checking on Whitford before we complete our deal," he mused. "I followed up by letter every lead he gave me. There weren't any local references because they've only lived in the city a few months, but the letters I got back were all tops."

"The thing that made me the maddest," Quig went on, "was the way she treated him, grabbing his front legs the way she did and making him yelp. Then saying they'd soon train *that* out of him, and that we'd coddled him too much. That made me boil. Probably I blew off too soon, but she made me so mad. I just can't stand that woman!"

"Well, you're in good company. Storm can't seem to stand her, either," Mr. Munson commented in amusement. "I must admit that I didn't get too bad an impression of her the night they were here. Oh, she's kind of a gushy type, but there're lots of women like that, and it doesn't mean they're bad, necessarily. What do you think of Whitford, Quig? Think he's a bad lot, too?"

"No, I kind of liked him," Quig said slowly. "I thought he was nice. His pipe smelled good, I guess. That's the only reason I can think of."

George Munson let out a chuckle and clapped him on the back. Quig turned red and began to laugh at himself.

"I know it sounds goofy," he acknowledged.

"O.K., it sounds goofy," Mr. Munson agreed, "and you and Storm detest the lady. Well, we'd better think this over again pretty carefully. Come on, Quig, I'll take you home in the canoe. The river's just like glass. Want to take the bow for me?"

They went down the long flight of steps to the dock, and Quig helped slide the sleek silver canoe into the water. Quig knew the water was mirror-smooth. There was scarcely any feeling of current as they headed downstream toward the Smiths' landing.

"Where did you learn to paddle so well?" George Munson wanted to know, as he watched Quig dip his paddle expertly into the water.

"At scout camp," Quig answered. "I took a special canoeing test last summer at Many Point. I like it next best to swimming."

"How's the free style coming now?" Mr. Munson asked, steering the canoe in toward the dock. "You going to win for us at the meet? I hear that's really quite an affair—big silver trophy cup and everything."

Quig shrugged. "I don't know," he said doubtfully. "I'm sure I can swim fast enough, but it's the raft problem. Keep your fingers crossed."

He crawled out of the canoe and waved his thanks as George Munson turned back upstream in the quiet evening. Up at the top of the steps he could hear Tommy clattering around, and somewhere up the little river he could hear the croak of the big old bullfrog.

Chapter 8

IN THE LITTLE VILLAGE OF SCOTT, JUNE RUSHED headlong into July.

"If only I could slow it down," thought Quig.

He had made himself a special calendar to keep track of the days before the swimming meet. The numerals were in braille on index cards, a separate one for each day, tucked into a holder that he'd thumbtacked to his bulletin board. When he went to bed at night, Quig took out the card for the day and threw it into the wastebasket. They were disappearing at an alarming rate.

This was Saturday morning, always a wonderful time at the Smiths' house. Quig's father was at home on Saturdays and they seemed to take on a festive, holiday air. Everybody got up late, and Dad waited until after breakfast to shave.

"The trouble with life," said Mother, "is that it's so daily. I don't remember who said it first, but it's true! On Saturdays, thank goodness, I can get off schedule and nobody cares." She always fixed something special for breakfast—pancakes, or waffles, or muffins.

But this morning was different from the ordinary run of Saturdays. Quig smelled just plain old toast wafting up from the kitchen, and Dad's electric shaver was buzzing in the bathroom. Tommy was tearing around getting ready to go to an all-day birthday picnic for one of his friends.

"Hurry up and get my breakfast, Mom. I'll be late," he was shouting down the stairs. "Is my present wrapped up?"

"All wrapped and ready on the hall table," his mother called back. "Come on down. Your breakfast's waiting for you."

Tommy thumped down the stairs, and Quig turned over and moaned. There was no pleasant anticipation for him as he looked ahead to the day. Mike had called swimming practice for ten o'clock, and the night before his father had announced that he was going along to watch. Quig had been speechless with dismay, and his mother had tried, very gently, to talk Dad out of it.

"You know, Jeff," she said, "I was really counting on your help in the basement tomorrow. It just has to be cleaned out before it gets hot, and I can't do it alone."

"Don't you worry, Helen," he reassured her, "we'll get the basement done. We'll have all afternoon."

Mother tried again. "What about the tomatoes?" she asked. "I thought you were planning to tie them up tomorrow, and work on the new trellis, and spray the roses. There's so much to do this weekend."

Quig listened with admiration. Mother never tried to boss Dad on Saturdays. She often said that it was his day and she didn't like to interfere with anything he wanted to do. This time, though, she was rooting for Quig. He grinned to himself, wondering how effective it would be. It wasn't.

"We'll all go to watch the practice in the morning," his father answered firmly. "It'll only take about an hour, won't it, Quig? Plenty of time to do all these things later, if we pitch in."

Quig had to admit that it wouldn't take much over an hour, so now he lay in bed dreading the day. The whole swimming team was working desperately to correct his problem with the raft, and now the time was so short. Dad was going to watch and no doubt kibitz, and it wasn't fair. Well, he'd have to get up and eat breakfast he supposed or he wouldn't be ready to swim at ten.

He dragged down in his swimming trunks and a T-shirt. Tommy had gone, and his father was outdoors doing something in the garden. He could hear him whistling. His mother put some cereal in front of him, and he reached for the sugar in its accustomed place, but it wasn't there. He felt around for it and tipped his orange juice over. A whole flood of the sticky stuff ran down onto his lap, and he jumped up, turning over his chair. Obviously this wasn't his day!

"Never mind," his mother murmured. "I don't blame you for being nervous, but you'll just have to pretend that you don't have an audience this morning. It'll be good practice for you."

"I'm not nervous!" Quig snapped at her.

She didn't say anything more, but went about cleaning up the spilled juice. Quig went upstairs to change into another pair of trunks, grumbling all the way. Fortunately he had more than one pair. He went back down to the kitchen and finished his breakfast in sullen silence.

About quarter of ten he slipped out of the yard without a word to anyone and went over to call for Mike. Don was there, too, so they walked down to the park together and swam out to the raft to sit in the sun and wait for the rest of the team. Quig

75

hoped that maybe his father would forget to come, but it was a vain hope. Peggy arrived with Liz and Joy and a few other feminine hangers-on; and above the shrill of their chatter, he heard his father's deep voice talking to his mother.

"Hi, Quig!" Dad called. "Let's get the show on the road."

Mike saved Quig from having to answer. "Hi, Mr. Smith!" he called back. "We'll be starting in just a minute. We're going through our whole routine, just the way it'll be at the meet."

Quig tried to calm himself. There was no real reason to be self-conscious in front of his father. He knew why his father acted as he did. And the other boys insisted that their parents were the same way with them. But his father fussed about such simple matters, like his running into furniture, or stumbling over thing outdoors, and a dozen other things that couldn't be less important. These were only the minor irritations of his blindness. The real dead ends in his life were important things like not being able to play baseball with the guys, and to leap onto a bike and speed off somewhere all by himself, or to take *River Girl* out alone and zoom across to the small island for exploring, and of course, there was the ever-present yearning to go down Dead End Bluff.

Sometimes Quig felt trapped, but as he grew

76

older he was doing everything possible to spring the trap. This race was one way to do it. If he could manage to win it, or at least do a creditable job, what doors it would open for him! He was trying so hard, and here was Dad, watching and making him self-conscious, and taking his mind off the target. It was maddening.

While Quig fumed on the raft, the "dress rehearsal" for the meet was going on. He gathered from the excited comments that Don did very well with his butterfly stroke, and Joe certainly had improved in the backstroke. The girls splashed in and out of their diving routines, gasping and giggling. Then it was time for the free style. He dived into the cool water and swam back to the starting point. Yesterday he had done very well. They had told him his speed was spectacular. Peg and Mike had been out of the race before it was half over, and Quig had finished with his hand on the raft and not an instant's hesitation.

Don acted as starter and blew a shrill blast on his whistle. They were off, and Quig almost forgot that his father was there, in the excitement of the race. Peggy was in great form, and he was hard put to it to keep up with her for the first round; but then she began to tire, and Mike was long since outdistanced. Quig kept up his steady, driving pace all by himself. He could hear his father's deep voice yelling a bass accompaniment to the lighter voices of his friends.

Quig made the turn for his last lap. He was swimming powerfully, and he thought perhaps he had never done it quite so well. His spirits lifted with each stroke, and he was sure that he knew now when to grab for the raft. Now was the time. Quig reached out just as his father's voice thundered above the squeals of the team, "WATCH OUT!"

He faltered and swerved past the raft. Silence fell on the beach like a wet, heavy blanket. He swam back, located his cane, and walked away without a word to anyone. He went along the path beside the small river, and behind him voices began to rise again, one or two at a time. No real words came to him—only the cadence on the soft summer air— his father's low, defensive rumble, and then his mother's voice, high and light, separating finally into a handful of words, "Jeff, I tried to tell you . . ."

He wandered on down the path and the voices were lost behind him. No one followed him. The sound of the river began to quicken between the high banks as it slid toward the rapids, and then he came to Dead End. He stepped over the white barricade on the other side. The water boiled in the rapids below him, and on beyond he heard the gentle roar when it plunged over the falls.

Quig didn't know how long he lay there at the top of the bluff, numb with the cold anger inside him. The birds that had fluttered away when he came, returned and went about their affairs, ignoring him. There was the muted sound of village life and boats on the river. He was scarcely aware of any of them; his mind was struggling with the thing that had just happened to him. So much confidence had grown within him this last week. Now it was gone—driven out in an instant of time. Perhaps he had better just ask to be let out of the race. Better to fail them that way than fail at the last minute and embarrass the team. Even if he did get his confidence back, how would he ever know that anything, just anything, might not disturb him.

The sun seemed to be reaching the top of the sky, for it was very hot on Quig's bare back. He got up and climbed back over the barricade and dragged slowly down Bluff Road toward home, white cane trailing dismally behind. Peggy didn't come out to see him as he passed her house, and he was relieved. When he went into his own house, he heard his father working in the basement and his mother in the kitchen. Quig climbed the stairs as quietly as he could, and closed the door to his room after him. He hoped nobody would notice that he had come home, but in just a minute his mother rapped and came in. She stood still at the door for a second before she spoke.

"Quig, you don't know how sorry I am. Mike told us that you've been hitting the raft almost every day this week. In fact, you haven't missed since Monday."

"Yeah, I thought I was all over this monkey business, but you see what happened when I got rattled," he answered.

"Oh, that wasn't it really," said Mother, "and you know it, Quig. If Dad hadn't called to you, it would have been all right. You were reaching for the raft. It was perfect. Dad realized it just too late. He feels terrible about it, Quig. You can't imagine how he feels!"

Quig was quiet for a while and then he said, "Mom, I guess I'll drop out of the race. It'll be better. I never know when I'm going to goof off."

Mother came over and sat down on the bed beside him.

"You're still mad at him," she said. "Don't be mad, Quig. I don't think he could help it."

She put her arm around him, and he didn't pull away. It had been a long time since he had let her do that. Now that sure, loving touch on his shoulders helped. They sat there, and he tried to sort out his mixed-up feelings. The icy anger was still there, but he found it hard to link it to his father, after what she had said. He was mad, all right, but maybe it wasn't Dad. It could just be that he was mad at himself.

"I guess I'm not mad," he said reluctantly. "At least I'm not mad at Dad any more. I shouldn't let things distract me when I'm swimming—that's it."

Mother took her arm away and spoke quietly.

"Quig, if I were you, I'd think twice before I dropped out. You're not a quitter; you never have been. I've watched you lick some big problems. I think you owe something to your team and to the village, too. We can never win that trophy without you."

Quig sat very still. He heard his father's step on the stairs. Mother gave him a quick hug and stood up.

"If you drop out now it will break your father's heart," she whispered.

Father was in the room. He made a sound as though he were about to speak, but no words came. He tried again, and this time he succeeded.

"I didn't mean to, Quig. It just slipped out. You were doing a great job! If you want me to, I'll just stay home the day of the meet."

All the resentment left in Quig began to break up. In a flash he realized what that apology must have cost his father.

"Well, you won't stay home!" he retorted. "If

you do, the race's off. Maybe we'll have to muzzle you, but you'll come. We were lucky this was just a practice."

"Imagine your father in a muzzle!" Mother giggled.

The others began to laugh, too, and then Father held up his right hand and said, "I solemnly promise not to say a word, Quig, not one single word all during the race, no matter what happens."

Quig held out his hand, and his father gave it a firm shake; then, feeling as though a great fresh wind had blown through the day, they all went downstairs for a sandwich.

Chapter 9

A LITTLE OVER A WEEK BEFORE THE MIDSUMMER
Meet, Quig walked down to the Munsons' after
breakfast, in a drizzly rain, his mind full of the free
style and the gorgeous trophy. He was to spend
the day with Storm and the puppies, while Mrs.
Munson took Freya and joined her husband in
town. Pete and Marcy were to spend the day with
Tommy at the Smiths' house.

"Turn about's fair play," laughed Dorothy Munson, as she put Freya in the wagon and started the
motor.

They were working on Freya's championship
again, now that she was back in condition following
the birth of the puppies. She was entered in an im-

portant bench show that day, and Quig, of course, was happy to take care of her infants. He gave Freya a good luck pat and went on into the house where Storm greeted him with loud enthusiasm. The puppies had been given their early feeding, so there wasn't anything for Quig to do immediately. He took Storm and went out to the shed to see them, anyway. After a romp with all six, Quig sat down on the floor and held Viking in his arms. Signe stood by, whimpering jealously.

"Never mind," he soothed her, "your turn will come all too soon. When Viking's gone, you'll get it all."

She climbed up onto his lap and pulled at his arm with her paw. Quig had to laugh in spite of himself. She behaved exactly like her father, who always pawed for attention. Storm had curled up in a corner of the shed and gone to sleep in sheer boredom. Quig suspected that he found his offspring very tiresome these days. But suddenly the dog was awake and on his feet, exploding into furious barking.

Quig's own sensitive ears hadn't detected a sound, with the romping puppies and the shed door closed against the rain. Now he hurried to open it and listen. A faint smell of gasoline hung in the wet air. He clutched at Storm's collar as the dog tried to push past him, and just then he heard a man's steps on the flagstones, followed by the tap-tap of high heels. The woman's heavy-sweet perfume drifting to him through the rain told him who it was before Mr. Whitford spoke. This time he didn't sound as pleasant as Quig remembered.

"Oh!" he said, "You gave me a start. I didn't expect to see anyone. Mrs. Munson said she was going into town."

Storm pressed hard against Quig, the deep, almost imperceptible growl vibrating in his throat. Quig was on guard, too, with an instinctive wariness.

"Mrs. Munson has gone into town," he said politely. "I'm in charge for the day. Is there anything I can do to help you?"

"We've come for our dog," said the man, the suave note creeping back into his voice. "Is he ready to go?"

"It's strange that Mrs. Munson didn't say anything to me about it before she left today," said Quig, quite as smooth as Mr. Whitford.

"Well, actually she didn't know anything about it," the woman spoke up in her high-pitched voice that Quig found so irritating. "Mr. Whitford went to Mr. Munson's office to make all the arrangements this morning, and he said his wife wouldn't be at home. They're going to send the papers and things on to us."

"That's right," Mr. Whitford agreed. "I gave

him a check for Viking, and he said for us to come right out and pick him up. We're in a great hurry, you see. We're all packed up and ready to leave for California right now. D'you mind if I just go in and get him."

Quig's mind was working in great leaps. He couldn't let Viking go without Mr. Munson's permission. The Whitfords' story somehow didn't quite hold together. Storm's dislike was too genuine, his own suspicion too deep. He would have to stall them until he could reach Mr. Munson on the telephone.

"Certainly you can get him," he said, struggling to keep his voice steady. "I'll go into the house and bring out his collar and a leash. You'll need food for him, too. I'll be right back."

He took Storm with him, almost dragging him by his collar. As he opened the door, he heard a snatch of the conversation between the man and woman, "—blasted blind boy—would have to be here!" the words floated to him through the rain.

His suspicions instantly jelled. He left Storm growling by the door and fell over the furniture getting to the phone. He dialed for information with shaking fingers. Once he had Mr. Munson's office number he was talking to his secretary in a matter of seconds.

"No, Mr. Munson isn't here," she said. "He went

out to the dog show about an hour ago. He was to meet Mrs. Munson there . . . No, nobody has called about the puppy, or been here . . . I don't expect him back all day . . . I'm sorry. Can I do anything?"

No, she couldn't do anything. He would have to do it himself, and it would have to be quick and sure. Now Storm was barking wildly, and Quig in desperation threw all caution to the wind. He rushed to the door and flung it open. Storm streaked out, as Quig had known he would. But Quig sensed at once that it was too late. The smell of gasoline hung heavy on the air again, and there was the sound of a car racing down Bluff Road.

Quig's heart pounded so hard he could scarcely breathe. Maybe everything was all right. Maybe they had been frightened away, and Viking was safe in the box with the other puppies. But even as he tried to reassure himself, he knew that Viking wasn't there—he would go to the shed and find him gone. He stumbled through the drizzle into the small kennel. The door was open.

"Viking!" he cried.

No delighted whimper greeted him. No furry little body flung itself against his leg. Viking was gone. Quig stood in anguished silence, unable to accept what his senses told him. After a few seconds something else began to penetrate his benumbed mind. He was standing in the shed surrounded by absolute stillness. There were no puppy noises at all. No Signe came begging for attention; there was no familiar clamoring for the mid-morning feeding. A staggering suspicion flashed into his mind. He fell to his knees and crept over every inch of the floor, making a sound that was more a sob than a call, fumbling with his hands, searching for the puppies. Finally he had to accept the dreadful truth. They were gone, all of them. The shed was empty.

Storm came in and Quig threw his arms around the dog's neck. His hair was wet and muddy; his tightly curled tail, for the first time since Quig had known him, hung limply between his legs. He obviously had chased the car until it was lost to his sight. Quig sat for a minute with his head pressed against the wet fur, trying to think, almost overcome with shock. Then he got to his feet and stumbled across the soggy lawn and into the house. He called the police, telling them as quickly as possible what had happened.

"They're on their way to California," he said. "The man claims his name is Whitford, but now I doubt it. They're driving a late model Ford, I'm pretty sure, but I couldn't get the license because I'm blind. The puppies were in a big wooden box— what do they look like? Oh, something like a cross between a German shepherd and a husky, I'm told."

Limply he shut Storm in the kitchen, locked the

door and started for home. His cane tapped mechanically along the wet sidewalk, and he turned into his own yard without consciously thinking about it. He was silently praying that his mother would be alone. He didn't want to tell her about it with the children around. Luckily they were playing in the basement.

"The pups are gone," he said abruptly. "The Whitfords stole them, all of them. I called the police. What shall we do now?"

His mother listened in shocked disbelief, then went silently to the phone. She called the Auditorium where the dog show was being held and had George Munson paged. In a few brief sentences she outlined the situation and listened while he talked. Quig stood beside her, tight with apprehension.

"That's exactly what I think," he heard her answer. "Oh, she did? That's perfectly wonderful—one bit of brightness in the gloom. We'll expect you late, then. I'll have the coffeepot on—I'll tell him. Good-by."

Mother walked over to the sofa and sat down. "Sit down, Quig," she suggested.

Quig stood in front of her, impatiently rejecting her invitation. He wasn't in a sitting down mood.

"What did he say?" he demanded.

"Well," said Mother calmly, "he was shocked, naturally, but he said you are not to blame yourself in any way. That you did exactly the right thing. He thinks your prompt call to the police will probably get the puppies back quickly."

Quig thought this over in silence and then asked forlornly, "What did you say was 'wonderful' and a 'bright spot'? I can't imagine, at such a time!"

"Oh, that!" Mother exclaimed. "Freya has won first prize in her class—I can't remember what it is called. So this afternoon she will go into the Winner's Class. If she wins there, she will go on this evening to compete for Best of Breed, and goodness knows what else. They may be quite late getting home, but they'll come directly here. We'll put the little ones to bed, and they'll spend the night if George and Dorothy are too late."

"Didn't he think it was my fault for leaving the puppies and going into the house while the people were there?" Quig asked anxiously.

"Of course not," his mother assured him. "He said it was very smart of you to think of calling his office. He's going to call the Scott police right away and make sure they've alerted other police around the state, and on west. Oh, by the way, he wants you to go down and feed Storm tonight, and says you may bring him up here if you want to."

The Munsons came home quite late, bringing a tired Freya who had completed the points for her championship and crowned the day by winning

Best of Breed. Quig had insisted upon staying up, so they sat and talked far into the night.

"I have to blame myself," Quig persisted. "If I could have seen the license! Or if I had stayed out in the yard with Storm. They would never have dared to take the puppies then. Storm would have torn that man to pieces."

"If, if, if!" exclaimed Dorothy Munson. "If I had realized there was something phony going on this morning when he called to ask if anyone was going to be at home! He probably knew all along about the dog show and assumed we'd be going. But I never suspected him. He was so smooth and plausible. After all, we were doing business with them."

"That's just it," George Munson groaned. "If we had just paid attention to Storm when he saw the Whitfords, especially that time the woman came alone. He tried to tell us we shouldn't be doing business with them. I've never known him to be wrong about people—he has an uncanny sense. Your trick to get to the telephone was clever, Quig."

Quig brightened a little.

"Well, I was really suspicious by that time, and I certainly wasn't going to let Viking go without checking with you. Storm kept on kicking up such a fuss, too. Oh, if I had only left him loose in the yard when I went in . . ." he hesitated, and then went on, "but I didn't dare. I think he would have eaten her alive. He hates that woman, as much as I do!"

The Munsons decided to go home, leaving Pete and Marcy asleep upstairs at the Smiths'. Mr. Munson touched Quig's shoulder as he went out.

"Now, you stop worrying and get some sleep," he ordered. "If you hadn't been there, we'd have had no idea what did happen to them. We'll have them back in no time. Every police officer between here and California is looking for them by this time."

Chapter 10

THE NEXT MORNING QUIG FELT AS THOUGH HE had lived through a horrible nightmare. He couldn't believe the puppies were really gone. He was sure he'd get up to find them safe with Freya in their big warm box. He knew better by the time the Scott police came to see him, however. They sat on the shady front porch and asked endless questions.

"Tell us all you can about the Whitfords, Quig," urged Officer Barry. "You think they were driving a late model Ford. How d'you know? The Munsons said they couldn't remember for sure."

"I'm quite sure it was a Ford," Quig replied. "You see, I've trained myself to notice sounds of motors. They're very different, you know. I can always tell the sound of Mr. Munson's boat on the river, and our boat, and the Harrigans' cruiser, and our car."

"You can!" exclaimed Officer Barry, obviously impressed. "And now, what did the people look like?"

Officer O'Brien cleared his throat in embarrassment. "That was sure a stupid question, Claude!" he objected. "How could you expect him to know what they look like? He can tell the sound of motors, but he's not superman."

Quig was secretly amused, but he said quickly, to cover the awkward pause, "Well, I really can't tell you that, but maybe my mother could. She saw them once."

Mother was just coming onto the porch with a tray of iced tea. She gave each one a glass and sat down in the swing beside Quig to drink her own.

"Yes, I saw them," she agreed. "The woman was a little thing, rather pretty, actually—blonde hair, blue eyes . . ."

"Huh!" Quig snorted contemptuously. "She may look pretty, but she certainly didn't sound pretty! She has the nastiest, whiniest high-pitched voice I've ever heard. It set my teeth on edge the first time I ever heard her speak, and she uses awful perfume. It's sticky-sweet, sort of, and heavy. Ick!"

The men laughed at that and got up to go.

"Thanks for the tea, Mrs. Smith, and for the information, Quig," said Officer O'Brien.

"Yeah, we'll go around sniffing at all the ladies'
perfume," Officer Barry chuckled.

"You can laugh," protested Quig, laughing a little
himself, "but Mrs. Whitford came to the Munsons'
twice after the first night we saw her, and each time
I knew her by her perfume. Ugh, I hate it!"

"We aren't laughing at you, Quig," Officer
O'Brien apologized. "It's just funny to think of
Officer Barry, here, going around sniffing perfume.
By the way, was there anything special about Mr.
Whitford that we should know?"

"Oh, he's tall, dark and rather handsome," Mrs. Smith remembered.

"And how did he smell, Quig?" Officer Barry wanted to know.

"Like a pipe," said Quig. "He always had one going, and he sounded smooth, if you know what I mean."

The men departed, and Quig followed his mother into the house to get ready for swimming.

"Mom, I still wish I could have seen the license plate. They'd have had more to go on. This way it could be just any Ford."

He practiced an hour or so with the team, but his heart wasn't in it. Afterward he spent most of the day wandering aimlessly around the house and yard, trying to avoid Tommy, who kept singing, "Oh where, oh where has my little dog gone?" until Quig felt like choking him.

Mike and Don and Joe came over and settled down to hear the story, and it was plain agony for Quig to go into all the unhappy details again.

"I'll bet they're halfway to California by now," mused Mike. "Probably drove all night."

"Yeah," agreed Joe, "but it's funny the cops didn't catch 'em. If they set up road blocks and all."

"Gee, there're a lot of back roads they could go on," objected Don. "You can't expect the police to watch every road in a dozen states."

"D'you know what I think?" declared Quig unexpectedly after a long silence. "I don't think they ever intended to go to California at all. I believe they're still around here somewhere."

"How crazy can you get?" Mike rumbled in his big, deep voice. "What would they stay around here for? Everybody's looking for 'em. They'd have to hole up somewhere, and where could they hide? It isn't like Chicago or New York or some real big city."

"And they told you they were going to California," Don reminded him.

"That's just it!" Quig exclaimed. "They made such a point of going to California—even the morning they stole the puppies. Doesn't that seem kind of silly, to tip everybody off, if they really meant to go there?"

That evening the family sat on the porch, cooling off. Quig heard a car stop at the curb, and George Munson came up onto the porch with an officer from State Police Headquarters. He wanted to know exactly what the Whitfords had said about their destination.

"He said they were in a hurry to get Viking because they were on their way to California. He said he'd been to see Mr. Munson and asked permission to pick him up," Quig answered. "But I don't believe they've really gone there. I believe they're hiding around here somewhere and waiting until all the excitement dies down so they can get away without being picked up."

"You have a point about California, son," replied the officer. "In fact, that's what we think ourselves; but you're wrong about their hiding around here. We think they probably talked California, but went off somewhere else, as far as they could go. After all, it's hard to conceal six yapping puppies. No, they're a long way away by now."

"Maybe you're right," said Quig thoughtfully, "but I have to have more time to think about it."

George Munson spoke up then. "You see, Quig, in order to make this profitable, Whitford will have to sell the pups for a good price, and elkhounds are so rare around here that he could never do it. They'd be spotted immediately. He may have taken them to Chicago. There're several good-sized elkhound kennels there."

"What about the pedigree?" asked Quig's mother. "Wouldn't he have to have that in order to sell them for any kind of price?"

"He copied the pedigree, word for word," Mr. Munson reminded her. "I guess I was pretty naive about this whole deal. Forging them will be a simple matter for a pro."

"Quig's worried because he couldn't get the license number for you, Officer," said Mr. Smith, who had been listening quietly. "How serious is that, anyway?"

"It really doesn't make much difference," was the reply. "If an officer had been there the minute they took off, it would have helped, but an experienced operator makes short work of changing plates. Don't worry about that, Quig."

"You know, I don't want to overlook anything," said George Munson in a thoughtful voice. "I didn't pay attention to Storm when he tried to warn me, over and over again, about these people. And I don't want to make the same mistake with Quig's idea. He's been pretty shrewd about the Whitfords. Maybe he's right about their being holed up around here somewhere. Anyhow, it wouldn't do any harm to run an ad in the state papers, would it?"

The officer agreed that it wouldn't, so the next evening the ad appeared in the *Scott Weekly Herald:*

GENEROUS REWARD for information leading to the arrest of persons involved in theft of six elkhound puppies morning of July 14 from George Munson, 28 Bluff Road. Man and woman escaped in late model Ford. Call BL 2-3348

No one responded with any solid clue. No one, apparently, had noticed a strange car fleeing through the village that dark, rainy July morning. No one had discovered the whereabouts of Viking and Signe and the four other baby elkhounds. Many people called the Munsons with false alarms or helpful suggestions. Mr. Munson tracked down every single lead, often taking Quig with him, but there was no trace of the missing pups.

The hot, humid July days dragged along. With no job to take up his time now, nothing but a sort of nagging sense of failure, Quig's spirits were at low ebb. He made a valiant effort to keep his mind off the lost puppies, and on the up-coming swimming meet, but it was very hard. No matter what he was doing he found his mind straying to them. Who was taking care of them? Was anybody loving them? He was sure the Whitfords would waste little time on that if they still had them. He remembered Viking's startled little yelp the day Mrs. Whitford had lifted him by his front paws. And as the days went by he clung stubbornly to the notion that they weren't far from Scott.

"I thought women were the only ones who were supposed to have intuition," his mother teased one day. "You haven't a thing to go on but your intuition. Where could they possibly be hidden around here? Everybody has been looking high and low for them. There aren't any places left."

Quig shook his head in discouragement. "Probably you're right," he agreed. "I guess it's just that those puppies would drive that woman crazy if she had to be shut up with them for long. She just didn't like dogs. And I can't imagine her making a long trip with six pups. Of course every place I can think of has been covered, except maybe the river. Did you ever think of the river, Mom? That's where they hid Moses, come to think of it."

He laughed at his own feeble joke, and then he stopped laughing and jumped to his feet.

"I don't think that's so much of a joke after all," he cried. "Why wouldn't that be exactly the place they might head for? The river's so huge—there are all those bluffs and caves on the banks, and there're islands, dozens of islands. Why couldn't that be it?"

He hunted around for his cane and hurried out.

"Where in the world are you going?" called his mother. "You can't go on the river by yourself."

"Of course not," Quig called back, already half way to the corner. "I'm going to the police station."

Officer O'Brien was there and glad to see him.

"Come in, come in!" he said heartily. "Got any fresh clues for me today? Get a whiff of the lady's perfume somewhere?"

He laughed and clapped Quig on the back. Quig ignored the humor and said excitedly, "I haven't got any actual clues, sir, but I've got an idea. Nobody's looked for them on the Mississippi. What about looking there?"

"On the river!" echoed the policeman, and Quig began to feel a little foolish and embarrassed. He wished he hadn't rushed off to headquarters quite so impulsively, but he stuck to his guns.

"I think we should look around there," he said stoutly. "There are all those caves, and islands and all kinds of places along the shore."

"Oh, sure," Officer O'Brien answered sceptically. "And we could maybe go on an excursion all the way down to New Orleans, all expenses paid. Nope, I can't see that, Quig. If we ever do find them, I don't think it will be there."

"Collision of two cars at the intersection of Willow Street and First Avenue," the radio chattered.

"Good-by Quig. Keep on thinking," Officer O'Brien urged. "Come in again."

He grabbed his cap and dashed out to the squad car. Quig trailed out the door and started for home, quite deflated. Officer O'Brien's words kept coming back to him, "If we ever do find them . . ." That was the first time Quig had ever seriously entertained the thought that they might not find them. Mr. Munson had always seemed so sure. Had he just been putting on a good front so that Quig wouldn't feel hopeless?

After lunch Quig phoned Mike and persuaded him to canoe for a while. The river was a little choppy, with a fresh breeze blowing, so Mother insisted upon watching them from the shore.

"I don't know what she thinks she could do, if we did capsize," grumbled Quig.

They got the canoe into the water and paddled out into the current. Quig hesitated to tell Mike what was on his mind for fear he would be laughed at. As a matter of fact, he felt like laughing at himself because they weren't allowed to go out of sight when they canoed alone.

Fat chance of finding the puppies within sight of our dock! he thought.

To Mike he said abruptly, "Let's go back. I'm hot. Besides, it's time for swimming practice."

So they paddled back, beached the canoe, stopped for Don and Joe and went down to the park. They swam for a long time in the cool water; and afterward, lying on the raft to dry off, Quig decided to tell the gang about his idea. They didn't laugh. In fact, they accepted it with respect.

"Why didn't somebody think of that before?" Mike complained. "That's a swell idea, Quig."

Mike was his best friend and usually defended his point of view, but even the other boys approved.

"Well, it's a possibility, at least," Joe said, with more restraint. "If I were Officer O'Brien, I'd think it over before I threw it out."

"Let's take a trip down the river!" Don cried. "Gee, it'd be fun."

When Quig talked about it at home that evening, his father was polite, but Quig sensed the same scepticism in his voice that he had heard in Officer O'Brien's that morning.

"I suppose it could be," he said slowly, "but it'd be like looking for a needle in a haystack."

Quig finished his dinner and started down to the Munsons' to talk the matter over with them.

"If you come back soon enough, we might take *River Girl* and go down-river for a little spin," his father called after him. "Nice night for a boat ride."

It was a perfect night. The wind had died to a murmur, and the evening brought coolness.

Quig could hardly bear to go to the Munsons' now, much as he liked the family and the dogs. As he approached he heard voices down on the dock, so he walked past the silent kennel and down the steps. Storm and Freya heard him coming and charged up to meet him, whimpering their delight.

"Hi, Quig!" Mr. Munson called. "Those dogs do miss you, now that you don't come every day."

Quig came on down the steps with a dog on either side.

"I miss them, too," he said, "but I miss the puppies more."

"Of course you do, and it's only natural," Mrs. Munson sympathized. "They're the ones you took care of, and they're so helpless and cuddly, just like real babies."

Quig shuddered. "Makes me sick to think of them with that woman," he said.

"I know," said Dorothy Munson. "Sometimes I get to thinking about how puzzled they must be about the whole affair. Can't you imagine Viking searching and searching for you, Quig, and wondering why you don't come?"

"Stop it, Dorothy," her husband warned.

Quig swallowed hard and then he said, "It isn't Viking I worry about the most, actually. Sure, he liked me a lot, and we had fun, but he liked everybody. He was crazy about you and Mr. Munson and the kids and people who came to visit. Signe's the one who's really having a bad time, I'm afraid."

"Why do you say that?" George Munson asked curiously. "I thought it was always Viking with you."

"Well," Quig answered slowly, "it was, I guess —he's the smartest pup I ever saw—but the last couple of weeks we had them, Signe began to follow me around all the time and beg me to take her. Maybe you noticed. She's kind of shy with most people, but not with me. She's awful lonesome and scared, wherever she is."

Then he remembered what he had come down for and began to tell the Munsons about his idea. "Dad and Officer O'Brien think I'm crazy, but I'd sure like to look," he finished.

The Munsons both listened very attentively, and when he was through, Mr. Munson said quietly, "I'll speak to the police about it myself, Quig. It certainly wouldn't do any harm to take a boat and look around a little. We're getting nowhere right now."

"I've got to go," Quig said, suddenly feeling cheerful. "We're going out in the boat now. Maybe we'll bring the pups back with us!"

Father was waiting in *River Girl* with the motor running when Quig arrived at their dock. Tommy was beside him, and Mother was just climbing in.

"Thought you were never coming back," his father said. "We almost went off without you. Which way d'you want to go—up or down?"

"Down, I think," said Quig. "I don't know why, but I have a feeling that if they went to the river, they went down."

River Girl roared gently and leaped away from the dock.

"Let's stay near the shoreline," Mother suggested. "Quig can listen, and the rest of us will watch."

Father throttled down the motor and they slid along the edge of the river. It was such a lovely evening that the air was full of myriad sounds for Quig to sort out. There were inboards and out-boards, the spank of water skis, the shouts and laughter of people in boats and on shore, and the barking of dogs as they passed.

"You see, Dad," Quig yelled triumphantly above the noise of *River Girl's* motor, "with all these dogs barking along the river, nobody would ever notice a bunch of puppies yapping, the way they would in a town. This would be a great place for the Whitfords to hide."

"Yeah," his father agreed reluctantly, "but it would still be one chance in a million that anyone would find them."

Chapter 11

"If I live through the Midsummer Meet I'll have it made!" declared Quig. "Maybe."

He felt often that he was being torn apart, with something tugging at each arm. On the one side, the free style race—on the other, the lost puppies.

Saturday of the Midsummer Meet was crystal clear and hot. Even at six o'clock when Quig first awoke, he could tell that it was going to be a flawless day. The air had a curious dry sparkle to it that he could feel, without seeing the blue sky. It would be perfect for the swimming meet and the community picnic to follow. The whole town of Green Valley would come to Scott to cheer its team on, and to eat supper in the park. Next summer Scott would go over to Green Valley for the summer festival.

Early though it was, Mother was in the kitchen when Quig came down. She was beginning the picnic preparations. Tommy appeared a few minutes later and raced outdoors, letting the screen bang behind him. Father was trying to sleep, but he decided it was useless, with all the commotion, so he came down to help Mother with the ice cream. She had insisted upon buying an old-fashioned ice cream freezer so she could make "real ice cream—the kind my grandmother used to make."

Quig helped his father smash the ice for the freezer, in a burlap gunnysack. It was cool and lovely on the back terrace where the family assembled to crank the freezer. Mother had been frying chicken earlier, and it was cooling in the refrigerator. There would be fresh homemade rolls and potato salad. The Bradfords and Munsons would eat supper with the Smiths, and each family would supply its own chicken, but the other food would be shared. Peggy's mother would bring her special baked beans, Quig's favorite food, and Mrs. Munson had promised chocolate cake for everyone.

Quig tried to concentrate on the picnic instead of worrying about the race. Yesterday, at the end of the final practice, they had all agreed that that was the thing to do; but it wasn't working for Quig. He couldn't forget that he had missed the raft last time around.

At eleven o'clock his mother suggested that he eat a bite of something so he would be all ready to swim at 2:30, but he couldn't. His stomach felt all tied up in knots. He didn't even want to lick his share of the ice cream dasher. Mike came along, and they walked down to Peg's house and sat on the porch with her. She was very nervous. The boys tried to laugh her out of it, but the attempt failed.

"Leave me alone. I can't stand it!" she wailed, and ran into the house.

Quig and Mike sat on for a while in moody silence; but when Peggy didn't come out again, they left to find Joe, who usually could see the bright side of things. They all stretched out under the big maple tree on Joe's side lawn.

"We're not supposed to talk about the meet," he reminded them.

"I know it," sighed Quig, "but what else? Maybe you'd rather talk about the pups? That would be really great! Remember what I did the last time out to the raft, yesterday?"

Mike, who by general agreement seemed to be in charge of their team, took up the conversation. "You'll be all right today," he assured him, "but

I'd better remind you, Quig, that it will be different in the race. Nobody but Joe will be allowed to yell at you from the raft, and all the noise from the shore may be confusing."

"That's going to be the toughest part," Quig acknowledged.

Mike drifted away, and Quig went home to take a shower and put on his new navy-blue swimming trunks, a special purchase for the occasion. Dad was asleep in the hammock; Tommy was out somewhere hunting frogs, his mother told him. She was darning socks on the back porch and trying to stay cool and calm, but Quig could sense the tension in her. He thought it might be better if everybody just admitted being worried about the meet, instead of pretending.

"You're scared I'm going to lose, Mom. Admit it!" Quig exclaimed.

She was always honest with him. Now she sat still for a minute in her rocker and when she answered, all the strain seemed to have left her voice. She spoke quietly to avoid waking his father.

"I'm not afraid you're going to lose, Quig. Frankly I don't care too much whether you actually win or not. I care about how you do this race. I think it isn't the winning of the race that matters so much to you—it's that you swim straight at your target, and neither swerve at the last minute nor slow up. Do you see what I mean?"

"I see what you mean," Quig answered, and slowly much of the tension seemed to be draining out of him, too.

His mother put her darning in the basket and moved toward the house. As she passed him, she gave him a gentle slap on his shoulder.

"I won't complain if you win, Quig," she said with a chuckle that told him she was amused at herself.

He helped his mother pack the food into the picnic baskets, and herded Tommy upstairs to clean up when he arrived, filthy and wet from his frog hunt. Father woke up, and at two o'clock they walked along the river path to the park and found the Bradfords already there, with a table staked out for them. The Munsons arrived soon afterward, and in a little while cars began streaming in with the Green Valley crowd.

Quig and Peggy went down to the beach to find the rest of their team. It was 2:15. Fifteen more nerve-wracking minutes and the whistle would blow for the Midsummer Meet to begin.

The tadpoles, little kids under eight, would be first. Tommy could hardly wait to jump in and paddle off. Peter and Marcy were entering the race, too. Quig could remember how excited he had been when he was still a tadpole. How different your excitement was when you were almost fourteen! The three judges, two men and a woman from another town nearby, were taken out to the raft in a rowboat. The crowd gathered back of the roped-off area at the beach. A quietness settled over them in the hot, still afternoon. Even the popcorn man stopped yelling his wares. Then the whistle blew, and the starter shouted, "Ready! Go!"

Quig heard Tommy's special little squeal above all the rest as the tadpoles jumped in and splashed off for their race. All he could think of was a dozen little kids splashing in a gigantic bathtub. The noise was incredible—thrashing tadpoles, shrieking crowd: "Go, Green! Go, Green!" "Sic 'em, Scott!"

The triumphant shout by familiar voices told Quig that the Scott tadpoles had won. Don pounded him on the back and yelled in his ear that Tommy had come in second.

Green Valley took two in a row after that with the breast stroke and butterfly. All of Don's practicing only brought him in a poor third. Scott came back to win in the backstroke, and they managed to squeak by in three out of four diving events. Peg, Liz, and Joy all performed superbly. When Quig's great moment came at the end of the meet, Scott was leading Green Valley by a meager two points.

"It's up to you, boy," Mike whispered in his ear. "Peg and I don't stand a chance with Hanson."

"Yea, Hanson! Yea! Yea! Yea!" yelled the Green Valley crowd.

"Yea, Quig! Yea, Quig!" Scott roared back.

"Listen for Joe," Peggy reminded him. "I'll be close to you at first, but toward the end I'll probably fall back and won't be any help."

The crowd calmed down while the three swimmers from each team lined up near the starter. Quig hoped they wouldn't yell so loud that he couldn't hear Joe. He wondered why he'd ever entered in the first place.

The whistle blew and they were off, plunging through the water toward the raft. Chuck Hanson, Quig knew, was a strong, tall swimmer, and he had the advantage of being able to see where he was going; but Quig felt sure he was keeping up. Peggy was swimming beside him, lightning fast as she always was for the first hundred feet or so. Mike was thrashing along somewhere behind, spluttering a shout of encouragement once in a while.

Joe stood on the raft and yelled directions. As they approached the raft for the first time, Quig thought he was drawing ahead, and that he had steered a pretty straight course, so far. "Turn!" called Joe. They all flopped and raced back toward the starting line at the beach. Quig felt wonderful.

He had never been so fast before, nor so strong. The long hours of practice every day had paid off. He was going to win for Scott. He was at the starting line and turning to begin the last, hard stretch. The next minutes would tell. If he hit that raft true and straight, without losing momentum, he could join the swimming team at Jackson High and compete with anybody. If he didn't, this was the end. Suddenly Quig knew. This was not just a race for him; this was the first real trial of his life.

His legs drove him through the water as though they were automated. His arms reached out in great arcs to pull him nearer and nearer the raft. Peg had fallen far behind. He had no idea where Mike was. The two others from Green Valley were eliminated. He and Chuck Hanson were swimming alone, racing fiercely, neck and neck toward the raft. He could hardly hear Joe above the wild excitement of the crowd. Three points rode on this race.

"Yea, Hanson!" "Go, Quig! Go, Quig!"

Quig listened frantically for directions from Joe. He couldn't distinguish a thing. The sound waves from objects that often guided him away from collisions were drowned in the uproar. He was totally dependent upon his own sense of direction. They must be very close to the end. He had to pour on that tremendous burst of speed at the last! Would

he have the nerve? One second's hesitation and they were lost. Chuck was right there.

They must be within a few feet. Quig could feel Chuck surging ahead in that last frenzied moment. Quig lunged shoulder to shoulder with him again. Where was that raft? Quig gritted his teeth and braced himself, hurtling through the water. Suddenly he heard Peg's voice from behind, high and clear above the roar, "GRAB, QUIG!" At the same moment he could make out Joe's voice again.

His hand shot out instantaneously. He felt the rough, sharp edge of the raft. One of the judges reached down and pulled him up. Another one reached for Chuck. Quig listened for the victory shout from Scott or Green Valley. Had he won, or had Chuck? He had no idea. All he knew was that he had hit the raft full speed. He had not slowed up. He sat in the blazing July sun, breathing deeply,

listening. A curious stillness had settled over the crowd on the beach. The judges talked together in low tones.

Whatever the verdict was, Quig knew he had won his own victory. Scott could lose, but he couldn't, not now. To have won for his team, to have brought back the trophy would be the crown of his triumph, of course, but it wasn't necessary. He waited calmly for them to speak. The raft swayed as the judge who announced the outcome of events stood up.

"May I have your attention?" he bellowed through the megaphone. "The final event of the swimming meet, the hundred-yard free style, has ended in a tie."

A great sigh swept over the people, and the judge continued, "It is the opinion of the judges that Chuck Hanson of Green Valley and Quig Smith of Scott tied for first place. It is traditional in these Midsummer Meets that if any of the events end in a tie, both teams receive identical points. Scott was ahead by two points when this last event began, so it is my pleasure to announce that Scott has won the 1966 swimming meet, and the trophy!"

Now a wild victory yell went up from the Scott crowd. Joe rushed over and congratulated him. Quig controlled his excitement long enough to shake hands with Chuck Hanson before he plunged into the water and swam back to the beach. His mother and father were at the water's edge to meet him. All the rest of the town must have rushed to that spot, too, he thought. He was pounded on the back until it positively hurt.

The Jackson High swimming coach had driven out from the city where he was attending summer session at the university. He would award the trophy after the picnic.

"Great stuff, Quig!" he exclaimed, shaking hands with him. "You come and work out with us this winter, and when you're in tenth grade, if you keep this up, there'll be a place for you on the Varsity."

Quig was beginning to come out of his golden daze. "I guess Peg should really have the credit," he laughed. "When she yelled 'Grab,' that did it."

"Oh, no," Peggy protested soberly, "that didn't

have a thing to do with your winning. You were right up there, swimming like mad, when I yelled. I just hoped you'd hear me and maybe it would save you from bumping your head. You had it made before I ever yelled."

Once the excitement died down a little, Quig began to wish he had accepted his mother's invitation to eat lunch before the meet. He thought the time for the picnic would never come. It did, of course, but not until Quig was sure he was going to die of starvation.

"What's the use of being a hero," he said, "if you're a dead hero. When do we eat?"

Food finally came, and it was a feast—chicken and salad, rolls and baked beans. Last of all Mother passed the ice cream, and they had it with Dorothy Munson's luscious chocolate cake.

Quig sat back and groaned luxuriously, patting his full stomach. Then a lull came in the chatter of the crowd. He guessed that the swimming coach was standing up to speak. In a moment he heard the big voice boom out.

"Ladies and gentlemen and kids of Scott and Green Valley, it gives me pleasure to announce that after a year of gracing the village hall of Green Valley, this beautiful trophy has now been won by Scott. This is always the most exciting event of the summer, and the best part of it is that the trophy never stays long in one place. As Jackson High swimming coach, I'm willing to wager that it will change hands many times during the years that Chuck Hanson and Quig Smith are around to furnish such great competition as you saw in the free style this afternoon."

Quig turned red with pleasure. In a minute Mike would be going up to accept the trophy for the Scott swimming team, and it would be placed in the special case down in the village hall.

"Now I want every member of the Scott team to come to the front."

This was a little different than usual, but Quig thought it was a good idea. He went with the rest of the team to stand in front of the coach.

"Before I award the trophy, I want to remind you that the team from Green Valley did a fine job. They only lost the meet by two points. Stand up, Green Valley team, wherever you are."

That was a nice thing to do, thought Quig. The crowd clapped and cheered, and settled down for the climax, the presenting of the trophy.

"Now that you have all had a chance to see this trophy again," the coach continued, and Quig knew that he must be holding it high in his hands, "it is my honor to present it to the Scott swimming team in recognition of the magnificent contest. Mike Walker will accept the cup for the group."

The time had come. The crowd hummed with excitement.

"Thank you," Quig heard Mike say. "Thank you very much for the whole team and for all of Scott."

A wild cheering went up, and all the boys pushed forward to take a closer look at the cup. Above the noise, Quig heard Mike say, "Hey, Quig! Where's Quig? Oh, there you are. Here take this thing and have a look."

He held out his hands and felt the cool, smooth heaviness of the big cup settle into them. The team came even closer around him. They all wanted to handle it, but before he gave it up, Quig went over every smooth inch of it with his inquiring fingers. After it was locked in the case he wouldn't be able to do that. Last of all he found the place where the many names of the past winners had been engraved on the sides. Before it went into the trophy case a new line would be added: SCOTT VILLAGE—JULY, 1966.

In the cool of the evening the men and older boys played baseball. Quig was bat boy for Scott. This time it was Green Valley, 9-6, a wonderful game. Afterward the men of Scott and Green Valley set up the fireworks, which they always bought together for the Midsummer Meet. When the first stars flickered in the sky, it was time for the rockets and flares and Roman candles. Quig sat with his crowd on the grass, and they told him how each one looked; the thin line of light streaking into the the dark sky, and the glorious burst of stars following the bang.

"The stars are green this time," they'd cry. "Oh, they're beautiful, Quig!" or, "You ought to see this one. It looks just like gold and silver rain." Or, "This is the best of all—all colors!"

The bang that accompanied the "best of all" was no different from any other bang as far as Quig was concerned, because he couldn't possibly imagine what any of them looked like. The fireworks seemed to go on forever, and long before it was over he was bored and tired of sitting. He stood up and moved carefully toward the river, but the crowd was so dense that he kept stumbling over people. Finally he gave up and sat down again. In a few minutes he realized from the talk that he was in the midst of Green Valley families, so now it was a matter of waiting it out until the last rocket was fired and he could go home.

There was a buzz of voices around him, punctuated by the bang of fireworks. Quig sprawled on the grass, so tired from the race that he was half asleep in spite of the racket. Even so his sensitive ears went on sorting out sounds, and he heard two men, evidently a little way away, talking between blasts.

"Being over here in Scott makes me think of those pups that were stolen here not long ago," he said. "You saw that ad in the paper, didn't you?"

"What ad?" asked another man's voice. "I don't always read the ads."

"I don't either," said the first man, "but I happened to that week. A whole litter of elkhound pups were stolen and . . ."

Another rocket sizzled into the air and interrupted the conversation. Quig was wide awake now, hoping that the man would continue when the noise died away.

"And what?" the second voice wanted to know. "I never heard of elkhounds, myself."

"Well, I've heard of them," answered the other man, "but I've never seen one that I know of. They must be plenty valuable—owner offered quite a reward. What I started to say was that they knew a man and woman stole 'em, and I've got a notion I should have gone to the Scott police right away."

"What happened, Dick?" demanded the other man. "You're talking in riddles."

Quig sat up straight and listened feverishly for the man's answer. He simply couldn't believe his good luck. To think that he had sat down right next to someone who knew something about the puppies!

"Well, nothing, actually," returned the first

voice slowly. "That's why I didn't report it."

"Report what?" urged the other man.

The first man laughed and said, "I s'pose I might as well tell you, as long as I've gone this far. There's so little to it that I feel silly, and yet it plagues me, sort of."

Another blast of fireworks went off, and Quig waited in a fury of impatience, straining in the direction of the voices.

The noise subsided and the man began his story.

"The day they were stolen, according to the ad, I was trolling on the Mississippi along about sundown—had rained most of the day, and just cleared off. A man and woman came down to the shore, carrying what looked like a big wooden box between them. I was too far away to see what was in it, but they acted as though it was heavy. They put it in an outboard and took off."

"So what?" puzzled the other man. "They probably live on the river and were taking home a box of groceries or something else from town."

"That's what I figured," replied his friend, "but they went past my boat and just as they came opposite me, I'll be jiggered if I didn't think I heard puppies whining and yapping."

"Aw, Dick!" scoffed the other man. "How could you possibly? All the sounds on the river, their outboard making a racket, you trolling. You must have been hearing things."

"Yeah, but I had the distinct impression that there were puppies whining in that boat," he persisted. "I know it sounds crazy, but the more I think about it, the man and woman and all—it keeps bothering me. Wouldn't have given it a second thought if I hadn't seen the ad."

"Not a chance in a million," said the other man.

"All the same, I should have gone to the police," the man called Dick insisted, "and I would have if I'd had any idea where those people went, but they just disappeared."

Quig was on his feet searching for the man. "Excuse me," he cried, but in concert with his words an enormous burst of sound split the evening air. All of the remaining rockets soared into the sky and exploded in the grand finale. The crowd shrieked and whistled, and Quig's voice was lost in the uproar. The people from Green Valley surged toward their cars, and Quig found it hard even to stay on his feet.

"Wait! I want to talk to you," he shouted, but everyone was retrieving picnic baskets and sleeping babies, and tired, excited children. Nobody paid any attention to him, if he was heard at all. If he could just have talked to the man—have asked what direction the boat went—told him about his own ideas. The chance was lost in the swirling, mass of people on their homeward way.

Quig moved toward his own people, listening for familiar voices, his whole body throbbing with excitement. The first clue—the very first! Maybe it wasn't any clue at all. Maybe the second man was right and it was just a box of groceries, but Quig didn't think so; he wouldn't think so. He wanted to believe that someone had seen the puppies' big wooden box being put into a boat and taken away on the river. That would certainly back up his own thinking.

"Here you are!" exclaimed Peggy, close beside him. "We've been looking everywhere for you. Where in the world did you go? I want to go home, but not by the river. You know how I feel about the Dead End at night!"

Chapter 12

QUIG WAS WAITING AT THE POLICE STATION ON Monday morning when it was time for Officer O'Brien to come on duty. He preferred to talk to him instead of Officer Barry, because Officer O'Brien always listened with interest, even though he didn't always agree.

"Hi, Quig!" It was the familiar voice. "And what brings you out so early in the mornin'?"

Quig followed Mr. O'Brien inside and told him about the talk he had overheard at the picnic. "You see," he finished triumphantly, "I'm not the only one who thinks they might be on the river somewhere! We've got a clue at last. Now maybe you won't think I'm so crazy."

"I don't think you're crazy," Officer O'Brien assured him. "I just think you've got mighty big ideas. How d'you think we should go about hunting for those puppy-dogs on the Mississippi River? Just tell me that. If we put every police officer in the state of Minnesota on the river looking for them, we could hunt a year and maybe never see hide nor hair of 'em."

"I suppose so," said Quig, forlornly. "I wish that man, Dick, from Green Valley would come over and talk to you and Officer Barry. He could tell which way they went. It would help to know that, wouldn't it?"

"Yes, it would," Officer O'Brien admitted, and Quig detected a very slight change in his voice. Some interest and even a trace of sympathy had crept in. He was quick to press his advantage.

"Gee," he sighed, "if we were only a couple of years older, my friends and I could take our boat and go out looking for them ourselves; but we're not allowed to go out of sight of our dock. Of course, I know you and Officer Barry couldn't go. You're too busy."

"True," pondered Officer O'Brien. "We're awful short-handed as it is."

A silence descended on the small office. Finally Quig stood up and took his cane.

"Guess I'll be going," he said. "I just thought

maybe I'd better tell you what I heard Saturday night. I don't s'pose it will do any good."

"Wait a minute, Quig," said Officer O'Brien. "Let's you and me think about this a little more before you go rushin' off. As you say, it's a clue, and goodness knows we've had precious few of 'em on this case. Sit down."

Quig obediently sat, his spirits beginning to lift again. He heard the officer walking around, straightening things in the office, rearranging things on his desk. The phone rang and he answered it, and then he came to stand in front of Quig.

"I been thinking," he said, "how would it be if we took my boat on my day off this week, Wednesday it is, and got your friends and went out looking for those dogs. Would you like that?"

Would he like that! He was off to get the gang almost before the last sentence was finished.

"One thing more," called Officer O'Brien. "If we had a dog along, it might help us searching islands and caves. How about that Tornado, is he pretty good about tracking? Would Mr. Munson let us take him?"

"Tornado?" whooped Quig, turning back in a gale of laughter. "You mean Storm. Oh, he's perfectly marvelous at that. I'm sure Mr. Munson would let us take him. He's a born tracker."

He started out the door again, but once more

Officer O'Brien stopped him.

"Quig, are you sure that fellow's name was Dick? The one who thought he saw the Whitfords?"

"Yeah, it was Dick," Quig assured him. "I wish his friend had called him Mr. Somebody-or-other. Then we could look him up over in Green Valley."

"We can, anyhow, but it'll be harder," said Officer O'Brien. "The Valley's not very big—not as big as Scott, actually. There can't be too many Dicks who were at the picnic Saturday."

Quig was curious. "How would you start looking for him?" he asked.

"Well, there are several ways," the officer said. "I could get one of their policemen on the trail, but they're short-handed, too. If we can do it ourselves, it will be better. We might . . ."

"Say, I've got an idea," Quig interrupted. "Couldn't we take the Green Valley telephone directory and look up every Richard? That's what Dick usually stands for. The gang could do that."

Officer O'Brien agreed, and Quig hurried off, almost running in his excitement. Here was a break at last.

Mike and Don and Joe were delighted with the whole project. It was something to do now that the excitement of the meet was over. They gathered on

Quig's front porch that afternoon. Quig brought his typewriter out, and Mike supplied a copy of the Green Valley telephone directory. His aunt lived over there.

While the boys went up and down the pages looking for Richards or Dicks, Quig typed the names and addresses and telephone numbers on a card. When they were finished and Don counted the names on Quig's list, they were astonished to find fifteen Richards, three Dicks, and one Dickson.

"Where do we go from here?" Joe wanted to know. "We'll go broke if we call all these people long distance."

"I've got it," Mike cried. "Let's go over to my aunt's house and call from there. It won't cost anything."

So they walked over to talk to Mike's mother about it. She thought it would be all right, but she phoned her sister to make sure.

"Come by all means," Mike's aunt invited cordially, "but you'd better make it around dinner time, because that's when people are home." It was finally agreed that they would go the next day about five o'clock and there would be an outdoor supper before the calling began.

Late Tuesday afternoon the four boys and Mike's mother piled into the station wagon and drove over to Green Valley. It was north of Scott and a few

miles in from the river, but it took only twenty minutes of driving to get there. Before the car stopped in front of the house they could smell hamburgers grilling, and in a few minutes everyone was eating in the back yard.

Then the boys rushed to the telephone in the hall to begin the evening's work. Quig made the first call. A man's voice answered, and Quig was suddenly speechless with stage-fright. Then he found his voice and said, "Hello, is this Mr. Wilson? . . . Oh, is he there? . . . Yes, please. Mr. Wilson? This is Quig Smith from Scott. Would you mind telling me, sir, if you were at the Midsummer Meet last Saturday? . . . You were? Well, do people call you Dick? . . . I see. I'm trying to find someone in

Green Valley by the name of Dick who was talking to a friend about the elkhound puppies that were stolen in Scott a while ago. . . . Oh, no, sir! . . . No, sir, I certainly didn't mean . . . Please let me explain. This man called Dick thought he saw the people who took the puppies . . . Yes, that was it, and we want to talk to him about it. You didn't? . . . I'm sorry, Mr. Wilson . . . Thank you very much. Good-by."

Quig sat back and mopped his forehead. "Whew!" he exclaimed. "He was insulted. He thought that I thought he stole the puppies!"

The calls went on, each boy taking his turn in rotation. Some of the Richards hadn't been at the picnic, a few weren't at home, and none of them knew anything about the puppies. It took a long time, and it got pretty hot in Aunt Margaret's front hall. They were almost through, and it was Don's turn again.

"I guess I'll call Mr. Dickson Macauley now," he said, dialing the number.

"Hello, is Mr. Macauley there? . . . Thank you."

The conversation began as all the others had. Then Don's voice became excited and he began to talk very fast. The boys stopped lolling around the hall and drew into a tight little knot around him.

"Thank you, Mr. Macauley. Sure, we'll wait for you," Don said excitedly. "Good-by."

He hung up and started for the porch, the others close at his heels. "That's our man," he told them. "He knows your aunt, Mike, and he's coming over here to talk to us right away."

They went outdoors where it was cooler, and in a few minutes Mr. Dickson Macauley came walking up the front steps. He greeted them all in a voice that Quig recognized immediately and sat down to talk. Aunt Margaret brought iced tea, and the rest of the grownups joined the party. Mr. Macauley went over the whole story again.

"But I lost sight of them," he finished, "and had no idea what became of them. Besides, at the time I had no reason to wonder where they went. It wasn't until a few days later when the paper came out and I read the ad, that I remembered thinking there were puppies in that boat. As I said to Jerry that night, Quig, I've thought a dozen times since that I should have gone to the police with my hunch, but what did I really have to tell them? Nothing."

"Oh, yes, you did," Quig broke in eagerly, "or at least you do now. They've tried everywhere on shore, and now I've almost got them talked into thinking that maybe the Whitfords went to the river. Mine was just a hunch, too, with almost nothing to go on; but since I heard you talking, even Officer O'Brien thinks maybe it could be. What we especially need to know from you is whether they went up or down-river. You do remember that, don't you?"

"Why, sure," Dick Macauley replied. "No trouble remembering that. They went down-river. There're a couple of islands along in there, and that's where I lost sight of them."

Quig drew a long breath. "That's just what we wanted to know, Mr. Macauley. Now we'll be going in the right direction, at least, even if we don't find them."

"I only hope I'm not leading you on a wild goose chase," Dick Macauley said. "The box I saw may not have been puppies at all—it might have been a thousand other things. And even if it was the dogs, the people may very well have left the river farther down and picked up a car, you know. Besides, that was well over a week ago."

"No!" exclaimed Quig with the stubbornness that he had shown ever since he first thought of the river. "If they went to the river at all, they're still there. I'm sure of it. The puppies may even be pretty much alone somewhere. That woman just wasn't going to spend much time with 'em. And she's not going to be moving 'em around unless she has to. We're going to look for them on Wednesday."

Officer O'Brien was at Smiths' dock very early

on Wednesday morning. George Munson brought Storm down to go with them. He turned the dog over to Quig and stayed to watch them off.

"I understand Storm has a new name," he chuckled to Officer O'Brien.

"Well, I came close," said the officer. "Knew it was Cyclone, or Tornado, or some such."

"Maybe Tornado would be a good name," said Mr. Munson. "He is something of a tornado when he gets excited."

The other boys came hustling down to the dock, in the early morning light, each carrying a bag of lunch. They plopped themselves into the boat, waved and yelled good-by, and the Detective Cruise began. Storm settled himself happily on the seat beside Quig.

"When we get to an island, I'll let you have a run," Quig promised him, but he kept a firm hand on the leash.

It was a wonderful morning for a trip on the river. There was the promise of a hot day ahead, but the early hours were cool. Officer O'Brien's boat had a big seventy-five horse motor, much more thrilling than *River Girl's* small twenty-five.

There weren't many boats on the river—just a few fishermen, and Quig could hear the throb of a tugboat pushing coal barges up to the Twin Cities. A few minutes later they rocked in its swell.

They were several miles down-river when Mike called out, "Hey, there's a big island over there. How about stopping?"

Officer O'Brien throttled down the motor. "I s'pose we might as well," he agreed. "It's just as good a place as any to start."

He circled the island until he found a good sandy strip for landing. Don and Joe leaped onto the shore and pulled the boat up after them. In a minute they were all out and scrambling up the slope into the scrubby trees. Quig kept Storm on his leash, and the dog seemed to understand that he was responsible for the boy in some way. He walked along quietly at his side instead of straining ahead as he usually did when Mr. Munson had him out.

"How're you coming, Quig?" Officer O'Brien called back to him, and Quig laughed.

"Just fine," he replied. "I've got a guide dog without ever having him trained."

They roamed all over the rather big island, looking everywhere that people or puppies might be hidden, with no success. Once a startled doe leaped from under cover just ahead of them, with twin fawns close at her heels. The undergrowth was alive with the sounds of hidden creatures that they seldom saw.

"I promised Storm a run," Quig said finally, "I'm going to take the leash off for a while."

He unsnapped the chain from Storm's choke collar, and the dog was off like a racer. A frantic rabbit fled past them as they all sat down on the shore to eat candy bars provided by Officer O'Brien. The little animals of the island flashed by, and in the distance Storm barked gaily.

"D'you think he's found anything?" Mike asked eagerly.

"Nothing but rabbits and gophers and things," Quig said, laughing. "I'm sure he isn't trying to tell us anything, except maybe that he's having fun."

In a little while Storm was back beside Quig, dripping from a plunge into the river. He stood grinning, with his tongue lolling out of his mouth, while Quig snapped the leash back onto his collar.

It was time to leave the island and look somewhere else. This time they turned their attention to the shoreline and followed it for miles as slowly as they could, stopping now and then to explore a cool cave or climb steps up the face of the bluff after finding a boat moored at the bottom. These climbs were all useless, because they found nothing but pleasant small houses at the top with pleasant people who excused them for trespassing in their front yards. Each time they asked if the puppies had been seen or heard in the area, but with no luck.

At noon they found a clear spring gushing out of the bluff and sat beside it to eat their lunches. The afternoon came on very hot, but they went on exploring the little islands and big bluffs. At five o'clock when Officer O'Brien said they were at least an hour from home and must start back, even Quig was tired out and ready to call it a day. In fact, he was beginning to feel discouraged and almost inclined to agree with the grownups who had said "only one chance in a million," or "like looking for a needle in a haystack."

Chapter 13

OFFICER O'BRIEN EASED HIS BIG BOAT INTO SMITHS' landing, and Storm was the first one out. Quig found his family, with the Bradfords and the Munsons barbecuing steaks on the shore. Everybody was invited to stay, but Officer O'Brien had promised to be home in time for dinner, and the boys thought they'd better go on home, too.

Quig changed into swimming trunks in the boathouse and went for a quick swim to cool off. Peggy was dying to know what had happened and Quig suspected that she was more than a little envious of them.

"Well, as you see, we didn't find the pups," he said as they sat down to eat. "We had a lot of fun though, and I know an awful lot about the river that I didn't know before."

"You didn't find any trace of them at all?" Peggy said in disappointment.

"Not a trace," said Quig. "We spent the whole day looking, and all we covered were some dinky little islands and a few miles of shoreline. It wasn't a drop in the bucket. I hate to say it, but I suppose we've got to give up."

Nobody said, "I told you so." They all went on eating in sympathetic silence. Quig took a bite of his steak sandwich and sat chewing with his face turned toward the river before he finally went on.

"Naturally I was disappointed not to find the puppies. I was so sure we'd find them somewhere out there, but I did learn one thing. I learned that the Mississippi River is absolutely gigantic. Here I've lived right beside it all my life, and I never thought about how huge it is."

"It's perfectly tremendous," Father agreed. "And if you think it's big up here in Minnesota, you should see it down below St. Louis where it's miles across."

"Well," said Quig, "Now I know what you and Officer O'Brien meant when you said it'd be like looking for a needle in a haystack. We roamed around all day long—didn't even find a cabin or a barn or anything on the islands. That seemed funny to me. Why don't people live on any of 'em, Dad?"

"As a matter of fact, Quig, most of them aren't good for building on, but there are a few islands where people live. You evidently didn't go far enough to find them. There is one island about twelve, fifteen miles down-river where we used to picnic a lot when I was a kid. We knew the family who had a summer place there. They owned the whole island—it was a pretty good size—and we could go down to swim and cook our supper on the beach any time we wanted to."

"Gee!" Quig exclaimed. "We didn't see anything like that. It sounds like fun. Is the family still there? Could we go there sometime?"

"I don't know what's happened to the place," his father answered. "I haven't been down there in years. The family moved away from this part of the country quite a while ago, and I think they sold the island. It was a great place, though. You remember it, don't you, Helen?"

"Of course," Quig's mother said. "I haven't thought of it for ages, though."

All three families were silent for a minute, finishing their suppers. Eventually Pete and Marcy and Tommy took their cookies and ran off to play in the sand.

"You know," Mrs. Smith said then, "Quig's birthday is on the thirteenth of August. Jeff, you'll be home on vacation then. Why don't you plan an all day picnic down-river? You can eat on the island for old time's sake."

"That would be just dandy, except for one tiny detail," Quig's father said, laughing. "What about the people who bought the island from the Gilberts and are probably living in the house this very minute? Did you think of that?"

"Oh dear, of course not," she sighed. "You couldn't expect me to be that practical."

But Quig wasn't ready to let such a good idea drop. "Why couldn't we go anyway, Dad? We could go down-river and you could show us the island, even if somebody lives there. We wouldn't have to land."

"Who's 'we'?" demanded Peggy. "If anybody goes, I'm going this time."

"Sure, sure," Quig said, soothing her ruffled feelings. "But that's another thing. We can't possibly take everybody in the *River Girl*, and it wouldn't be any fun if we had to leave half the gang home."

"Go ahead and ask them all," George Munson urged. "The thirteenth is a Saturday, isn't it? I'll take the overflow in our boat. I've been itching for a good excuse to take her down-river on a real jaunt."

The Munsons had a brand-new white runabout with blue trim and two big thirty-five horse motors.

White Fawn and *River Girl* together could carry everyone nicely, so Peggy and Quig spent the rest of the evening making plans for the birthday. His mother would fix the food, and they would ask Joy and Liz and Mike and Don and Joe. They'd leave early in the morning and spend the whole day on the river.

The days before Quig's birthday dragged on. With the swimming meet over and still no word about the puppies, he found the days tedious and long. Everybody seemed to have given up hope of ever finding them, and even he was secretly more and more uncertain. Having the trip to anticipate helped.

The birthday morning came bright and clear after days of muggy heat. The party gathered at Smiths' dock, all wearing swimsuits and equipped with jackets, blankets, scarves and suntan oil. George Munson came flying along in his *White Fawn*, with Storm beside him. The baskets of food were quickly stowed away, and they were off on the river. The sun felt good on Quig's brown back as he sat with his father and managed the speed. *White Fawn* was loafing along beside them. Quig could hear the powerful, exciting purr of her motors. There was a gentle breeze blowing downstream, and a slow current.

Everybody was starving by the time the sun was high overhead, and they began to look seriously for the island. Just as they rounded a bend in the river, a little below Hastings, Quig's father spotted it.

"There it is," he shouted. "Let's see if we can find the dock. I think it used to be down at the other end."

It was a beautiful island. Peggy described it to Quig as they circled it slowly. There was a smooth sand beach at the end where the dock was, and just above it the house stood in a grove of great oak trees. The dock was broken and sagging, obviously

out of use for a long time. The house gave the same impression, Peggy told him. Everything about it was decayed and fallen into ruin. The porch screens were rusted out, the steps were broken, the windows were boarded up. The island sloped up from the back of the house to a rocky cliff on the other side.

Quig's father was delighted to be there again after so many years.

"Let's land," he yelled, over the rumble of the motors.

They fastened the boats to the rickety dock, and he was the first one ashore.

"Seems deserted," he called back over his shoulder, starting up the sandy path to the house.

Quig followed close behind his father with Storm at his heels, and the rest came along in single file. George Munson brought up the rear. They all tramped onto the porch, and it shook under them. Someone tried the door, but it was locked. They went down and around the house, pushing through the underbrush that had overgrown everything. Peggy kept close to Quig and Storm.

"I don't like this place," she said in a low voice. "It's spooky, somehow—so lonesome."

Mr. Smith heard her and said, "You should have seen it when the Gilberts had it, Peg. It was quite a place then. But it certainly has gone to ruin. We can go for a swim and have our picnic down on the beach, anyhow."

"We can go in. The back door's unlocked," shouted Mike.

He and Joe had run on ahead and were now in the kitchen of the old house.

"It's funny—the back windows aren't boarded up like the rest," Peggy commented as they followed the others in.

"My goodness, somebody must live here!" squealed Joy. "There's grease in this frying pan, and here's a can of milk open."

Quig stood still, sniffing the variety of odors in the musty air—bacon fat, coffee, and several others that he couldn't identify immediately. He was so used to orienting himself in new surroundings by sound and smell and touch, rather than sight, that he sniffed very curiously, now. Storm had been investigating the room with his nose, too, and suddenly he ran back to Quig and pressed against him. Even before he heard the dog's deep growl, he felt the vibration all through his body. At almost the same instant Quig recognized one of the smells that had been eluding him. It was the hint of a woman's perfume, heavy-sweet, hanging in the stale air of the kitchen. Incredible! She had been here, today. Quig alone, might be wrong, but not Quig and Storm together—not this time.

Nobody was paying any attention to them. The rest were all busy investigating the house they had thought deserted.

"Come on, kids, let's go!" called Quig's father. "We're trespassing."

"Wait a minute, Dad," Quig broke in quickly. "They've been here."

"Who've been here?" Jeff Smith demanded.

"The Whitfords," Quig answered. "I smell her perfume. I couldn't miss it. And Storm knows it, too."

"Oh, Quig, you must be out of your mind!" his father exclaimed. "You couldn't possibly tell by that perfume. Let's get out, fast. I tell you, we're trespassing. Somebody's living here."

"Sure," persisted Quig. "The Whitfords are living here. You said yourself there aren't too many islands with houses. If this house was deserted, why shouldn't they be here? It makes sense."

Quig felt Mr. Munson come close and touch Storm. "Wait, Jeff. We'll have to find out about this. They're both in dead earnest."

Peggy called from the front room, "This is funny. There're a lot of papers here on the table with the pups' names on them. Where do you s'pose they could have come from?"

George Munson hurried into the other room and was back in a minute with a handful of papers.

"Jeff, she's right. These are forgeries of the pedigrees. What do you know about that!"

"Sounds too much like a third rate movie to be true!" Quig's father exclaimed.

At that moment Quig heard steps on the walk and the perfume rushed at him. A well-remembered, whiny voice demanded, "What do you think you're doing in my house?"

Quig's friends shrank back and the woman moved into the kitchen, where for the first time she saw George Munson and Quig and Storm, who was growling fiercely now and lunging against the restraining hand on his collar.

"Get that dog out of here, I tell you. Get him out of here!"

She turned and rushed from the house. Mr. Munson released the dog and commanded, "Go, Storm. Hold!"

Quig heard Storm's flying feet on the steps and a frantic shriek from the woman. "Call off your dog before he kills me!"

"He isn't hurting you, that I know, and he won't, just as long as you don't try to get away," remarked Mr. Munson, calmly.

He followed Storm outdoors. Peggy whispered to Quig, "You should see Storm. He grabbed her arm, but he's just holding it. He hasn't closed his teeth."

"Now, Mrs. Whitford, may I inquire where my puppies are?" Mr. Munson asked. "I see you've been busy forging their pedigrees. No wonder your husband took such detailed notes the night you came to see them!"

"I'm not saying where they are," she replied in the whine that Quig found so infuriating.

Quig had followed Mr. Munson out of the house and now he stood beside him. He considered this very much his business. He could hear his friends whispering as they sat on the steps, huddled close together.

"It's just like a play," Peggy murmured.

"Yeah, or a mystery story," Joe suggested. "This deserted old house and the island and all."

The woman began to cry, and Quig found himself pitying her, to his disgust.

"I'm sorry I can't make you more comfortable," Mr. Munson apologized. "We'll just have to wait until you're ready to tell me about my puppies, I guess."

"You call off your dog or I'll sue you for assault," she whimpered. "You just wait till my husband comes back."

"Yes, that's what I intend to do," promised Mr. Munson.

One of the boys snickered.

"Let me go," sobbed the woman. "I won't run

150

away. Where could I run to? Just make this brute let go of my arm."

Mr. Munson considered quietly for a few minutes, then said firmly, "I'll call Storm off, Mrs. Whitford, if you tell me where to find my puppies, but not before. If they aren't here on the island, you must know where they are."

"All right, I'll tell you about the pups," she agreed, unexpectedly, "but I can't talk with this dog hanging on my arm."

Storm gurgled in his throat. "Down, Storm!" George Munson ordered.

The dog dropped the woman's arm and ran off up the slope in back of the house. Quig could hear him breaking through the underbrush. Mr. Munson ignored him and continued his conversation with Mrs. Whitford.

"Now, your part of the bargain. Where are my puppies?"

"The pups aren't here," she said sullenly. "You can see that. They're all sold, every one of them. Man from Chicago came and got 'em."

Storm came rushing back, barking wildly. He raced up to them and started off again. Quig was paying close attention to the dog's behavior. Now he stepped forward.

"That isn't true," he said boldly. "I'm sure they're here, somewhere on this island. You wouldn't have kept 'em in the house, or even near the house, probably."

All talk in the group stopped.

"How do you know, Quig?" asked Mr. Munson.

"Well, she hates dogs, so she wouldn't have wanted 'em underfoot, not six of 'em, and Storm has been trying to tell us that he's found something for the last five minutes. Just listen to him."

They listened. Storm was barking madly somewhere in the distance. Then Quig heard him galloping through the undergrowth, coming back to them again. He leaped around Mr. Munson insistently.

"I don't think he's after rabbits," said Quig. "I think he's found the puppies. Or at least he's found where they kept 'em."

"I tell you, they aren't here," the woman whined again.

But Mr. Munson was paying attention to Storm now.

"Something's certainly on his mind," he decided. "I agree with you, Quig. He's trying to tell us something."

"You go ahead with the youngsters," suggested Quig's father. "I'll stay here and keep track of our hostess."

"You're the only one who knows the island, Jeff," objected Mr. Munson. "I think you'd better go along with the kids. I'll stay here."

"I know," Peggy said. "Liz and Joy and I will stay here, and the rest of you go. As she said before, there isn't any place she could run to."

Then she thought the better of it. "Or maybe one of the boys better stay with us."

"I'll stay," volunteered Mike.

Storm was dancing around them, running off up the slope a little way and dashing back to Mr. Munson.

"Well, all right. Let's go," he agreed. "Storm will have a heart attack if we don't do something quick."

A deep inner excitement seized Quig. He stumbled up the slope, holding onto Storm's collar and letting the dog guide him over the rough ground. He was hazily aware of the sound of an outboard, far off on the river. The going became very rough, and his father put out his hand to help him, but Quig brushed him aside. He wanted to do this alone, with Storm. Now they were descending, scrambling down a rocky incline that reminded Quig of Dead End Bluff. He fell down, skinned his knee and scratched his face.

"Here's the shore," cried Don.

"I remember now," Jeff Smith told them. "We used to come down here and explore the cave. There's one that runs back into this hill. I'd forgotten all about it."

"How do you get to it?" Quig asked. His excitement was soaring.

"There's a narrow path at the bottom of this low cliff right at the edge of the water," his father said. "The cave opens onto the path."

Storm had pulled away, and Quig heard his feet sliding on the rocks. He stood still on a level spot and listened. The noise from the outboard was loud now, and the waves from the backwash were beating against the rocky shore. Storm exploded into barks again, and then the barks quieted into whimpers. From somewhere below came the sound of high answering whimpers, above the noise of the waves and the motor and the gentle wind. Nobody else seemed to notice—only Quig with his ears attuned to hear what he couldn't see.

"Look in the cave!" he cried. "Storm has found the puppies. I hear them."

The men jumped down onto the narrow path and started along toward the cave. Don and Joe scrambled after them and Quig stood waiting. If he had known how the cliff sloped, he might have tried to back down on all fours; but he didn't dare try. He was afraid of landing in the river.

"They're here all right," George Munson shouted. "I can hear them now, and Storm's wagging his tail like mad." Suddenly he stopped and called, "Quig, where are you?"

"I'm here," Quig called back. "Don't bother about me—just get 'em."

"I should say not!" exclaimed Mr. Munson. "Give him a hand, somebody. I want Quig down here with me."

Joe and Don ran back and helped him down, and he inched along, clinging to some bushes, until he came to his father and Mr. Munson. The clamor of the excited puppies was loud and shrill now.

"This was a smart place for them to hide the pups," said George Munson. "These bushes cover the mouth of the cave so completely that nobody on the river would ever dream there was one here."

The men pushed aside the bushes and the crude wire gate across the entrance. Storm plunged in, and the puppies tumbled out. Quig knelt down on the path, and they swarmed all over him. He heard Viking's distinctive little yelp of greeting, but it wasn't Viking who got into his arms first, it was Signe, crawling up to lick his scratched face with her warm, wet tongue, whimpering in unutterable happiness.

"Well," said Mr. Munson, clearing his throat, "They're all here, all six of them, and they act fine, but let's take them back to the house and see."

They climbed back up the cliff and set the puppies on their feet. Storm herded them down the slope to the house. During all the commotion of finding the puppies, Quig had forgotten about the boat approaching the island. Now he realized that there was no longer the sound of a motor on the clear air; it must have landed somewhere, or perhaps it had gone around the other side of the island and passed out of hearing. Signe was running at his heels, coaxing to be carried, and just as he bent to pick her up, a high, piercing scream tore the air. He knew that scream; it was the same one that had saved the race for him at the Midsummer Meet. Something was happening to Peggy. The scream was followed by a cry.

"Quick! Quick! They're getting away."

Then Quig heard the pounding of feet on the walk, the other girls yelling, Mike's deep voice shouting something. The men began to run, with Don and Joe close behind, and Storm tearing on ahead. Quig came along, carrying Signe, with all the other puppies trailing after. Suddenly there was the noise of an outboard again, near at hand, and then a roar as it sped away down the river.

"They've gone" wailed Peggy. "We couldn't stop them."

"Gee, I'm so sorry, Mr. Munson," Mike apologized. "There wasn't anything I could do."

Mr. Whitford had come soon after the searchers had gone to follow Storm. That was evidently the motor Quig had heard. He and his wife had gone

into the house, promising to come right out, but they had dashed out the front door instead, with a couple of suitcases, rushed down to their boat and escaped.

After he heard the story, Quig's father said, "Want me to go over to Hastings, George, and get the police on their trail?"

"No, don't go now," said Mr. Munson slowly.

He was sitting in the long grass, going over each puppy carefully with his hands. He put Viking down and sat still for a minute, then he went on, "I don't know what good it would do, really. We have the puppies back, and they're all in fine shape, apparently. That's what we wanted, wasn't it Quig? As far as I'm concerned, they can just go! But, of course, the police will want to know what happened. I'll call them when we get home."

"Well, whether they're caught or not, I never want to see them again," said Quig.

Jeff Smith came to Quig and clapped him on the shoulder. "One chance in a million, Quig," he said.

Chapter 14

Now that the puppies were back, the summer once again slipped into a comfortable pattern. Quig went every day to take care of them and have a romp afterward. Signe, he noticed, still adored him and tried to monopolize his attention, sulking quite noticeably when he played with Viking or the others. She seemed to be trying to tell him how miserable she had been while they were away. The four puppies that had been promised when they were little were taken away by their new owners quite soon, and after that the small kennel seemed unnaturally quiet.

An important elkhound breeder from New England was corresponding with Mr. Munson about Viking. He made an appointment to see him, so Quig had to face the reality of his loss. In fact, he was afraid that before many days there would be no more puppies in the shed. Signe would be gone, too, and Storm and Freya would be alone.

He still went swimming every day, remembering the coach's words, "Keep this up, Quig, and there'll be a place for you on the Varsity!" Sometimes he went along while the boys played baseball or tennis, but this was tiresome in the wave of smothering heat that spread over Scott the last of August. Quig preferred to go home for a glass of lemonade and an hour or so of reading. He had sent for a couple of talking books and some braille books from the state library. It seemed a good idea to brush up on his braille before he started ninth grade. It hardly seemed possible, but school would be starting again soon. The summer had been so short, and yet so much had happened. It was hard to figure. In many ways Quig was glad about school. It would take up his time when the dogs were gone and his job was over.

One hot evening the Bradfords and the Munsons and the Smiths picnicked together on the shore. Quig loved to fish where the small river cut its channel out into the big one. This evening he caught several plump crappies, and George Munson reminded him of the night in June when he cast and came up with Storm on his hook.

"Luckiest accident I ever had," Quig said, feeling around for the dog. Storm always tried to keep at a safe distance from his rod now, but he did enjoy being close to Quig.

Tommy was dredging along the edge of the river with a minnow net. He was still absorbed in his frog collection. He kept the frogs in an old dishpan in the back yard, covered securely with a piece of screen. They were mostly little green speckled things, but Tommy had never given up his determination to catch the "big old bullfrog" that lived below Dead End Bluff. He made countless trips to the bottom of the bluff in the daytime, but never a trace of the huge creature did he see. "Quig's right; I'll have to go at night, I guess," said Tommy. "That's when we always hear him. Guess I'll go tonight."

"Oh, no, you won't go down Dead End tonight or any other night!" exclaimed his mother.

"Imagine going down there in the dark!" shuddered Peggy.

Quig smiled to himself and thought that it would be just as easy for him to go down the bluff at night as it would in the daytime.

The night after the picnic, Quig's parents went with the Munsons and the Bradfords to have dinner in Green Valley. Quig and Peggy had been elected to sit with the three younger children and the dogs. Quig didn't really mind, as long as it didn't happen too often. His mother only suggested it when she knew she and Dad wouldn't be away too long.

Quig and Peggy ate their supper on the Munsons' lawn with the children after Quig finished feeding the dogs. Then they went back to Smiths' to spend the evening. They had been given strict orders to stay away from the water—no swimming, no canoeing, no fishing, and no boys.

"You and Peggy with the children is one thing, but with your gang, that's something else," his mother reminded him.

"This is going to be pretty dull," complained Quig. "What a night for canoeing! The river must be as smooth as glass. There's not a bit of wind."

"I know," Peggy sighed, "but I can see their point, can't you? It would be awful if anything happened while they're gone."

"Well, they've fixed it so nothing possibly can," yawned Quig. "D'you want to listen to my new talking book? It's not bad."

"Not especially," Peggy answered. "Why don't I go home and get those new records I bought the other day? You haven't heard them yet. I'll check on the kids while I'm over there, too. I think they're playing in our back yard."

"I hear them making a big commotion about something," agreed Quig.

She was soon back with the records and the information that the children were having a marvelous time in the yard. Quig brought the record player out to the porch, and they listened to Peggy's new records. But while she changed from one to another, Quig, with his uncanny awareness of sound, sensed a stillness in the neighborhood. Far off on the river he heard an outboard; a bird cried on the bluff; somebody in the distance was using a power mower, but there was no sound of children playing in Bradfords' yard.

"I don't hear the kids," Quig said abruptly. "We'd better look."

Peggy spun the record and a folk singer wailed on the still air. "Oh, they're all right. I checked on 'em just a few minutes ago. Listen to this."

"Yeah, real good," said Quig, "but turn it off a minute, will you, Peg?"

He walked down off the porch and stood listening.

"Tommy," he shouted. "Tom, where are you?"

No answering shout came back, just the faintest echo of his own voice from the bluff.

"Let's go," said Quig, coming back to the porch for his cane.

Peggy shut off the record player and followed

him down the walk.

"Where shall we look?" she demanded, hurrying to keep up with his long strides. "They certainly aren't far away. It can't be more than ten minutes since I saw them." She sounded a little anxious.

Quig was tapping briskly along the sidewalk toward Dead End Bluff.

"I think we'd better go to Dead End first. I've a feeling my little brother has some business there. Is it dark yet, Peg?"

"Not quite," replied Peggy, sounding puzzled. "It's only 8:30. It's just kind of dusk. It would be dark at the bottom of Dead End, though. What would Tommy be doing on Dead End Bluff in the dark, Quig?" Suddenly there was panic in her voice. "Oh, no they couldn't be there!"

"I'm afraid they could," Quig insisted. "We'll have to see," and as he spoke the big old bullfrog bellowed somewhere below the bluff.

"Tommy," he called again. They were almost at the end of the road now, where the bluff plunged down to the edge of the little river. "Tommy, are you down there?"

This time he heard voices, all jumbled together in excitement and argument. Then Tommy's voice, "I'm down here, Quig. I'm hunting my frog, but I don't want Pete and Marcy to come down. Make them go back. They don't know all about the bluff

164

the way I do."

"Tom Smith," Quig commanded sternly, "you come back up that bluff this minute, do you hear? Pete and Marcy, you come back *immediately!*"

"We're coming, Quig," Pete responded meekly. "We only went halfway down. We're coming right up."

Quig heard them puffing, and the sound of their feet scrambling on the rock steps. In a minute they were at the top, and Peggy was pulling them over the barricade.

"Tommy," Quig shouted furiously, "if you aren't on your way up by the time I count to ten, I'm coming down after you." Even as he said the words, the familiar thrill of fear and anticipation tingled through him.

"Ho, ho!" laughed Tommy at the bottom of the bluff, "You've never been down Dead End in your life. Daddy won't let you. I'm gonna stay down here till I get my big old frog. He's here. I can see him with my flashlight, and I'm gonna get him."

Above the swishing of the rapids and the remote murmur of the low falls, Quig heard Tommy's feet slithering around on the rocks at water's edge. He sucked in a big breath of air and began to count.

"I'm at nine, Tommy," he called. At the same time he began to take off his shoes. He could feel the way better with his bare feet.

"You can't go down there, Quig," Peggy wailed. "You'll break your neck. If it weren't so dark, I'd go, but I can't go in the dark. I just can't, Quig. You know I can't go down Dead End in the dark!"

"Ten!" counted Quig and threw his leg over the barricade.

"Don't you come down here!" screamed Tommy. "I'm getting my frog. He's sitting on the next rock. I'm getting him with my net."

Quig was over the edge now, fumbling for the first foothold. He was going down with his stomach flat against the bluff, feeling for support with his fingers and toes. He tightened his muscles, trying desperately to still the trembling in his body. There was a sudden silence from below, then a hoarse croak from the enormous bullfrog, and the clatter of metal against stone. Simultaneously Tommy's voice rose in a high, thin shriek of pure terror.

"Quig, I've dropped my flashlight. It's pitch dark. I can't see! I've got my frog, but he's trying to get away."

"Don't move. I'm on the way," Quig called. His voice sounded more confident than he felt. Then he smiled to himself. It was a lucky thing Dad wasn't here. The thought somehow braced his nerve. He could do it.

Peggy was standing at the top, making distressed, helpless noises. Tommy below was moving on the rocks, and there was the thud, thud, thud of the frog's heavy body struggling to get out of the net. Suddenly he heard Tommy lurch. There was the sound of sliding stones, a frightened panic-striken yelp and a splash into the water.

"Quig, I fell in. The current's pulling me out. I can't touch bottom!"

"Grab a rock and hang on!" Quig ordered. "I'm coming. Peg, go for help, quick!"

Peggy was evidently too terrified to answer. Pete and Marcy were squealing, though. He heard the sound of racing feet as Peg rushed down Bluff Road. Quig continued his slow, painful descent. He had always planned to explore Dead End Bluff some day, but never like this. It was to have been a great, triumphant moment, the symbol of victory over his blindness. But this wasn't like that—it wasn't something anticipated safely and calmly from the other side of the white barricade. It was something he had to do and he was doing it even though he was scared stiff.

"Tom, are you hanging on?"

"Uh-huh, I found a place. Hurry!"

Tommy was down there, alone in the dark, fighting to hang on in the turmoil of the rapids. Quig was going down to save him from drowning, not to prove anything to himself or his father or anybody else. The noise of the rushing water was much louder now, as he dropped with desperate slowness down the face of the bluff into the miniature gorge.

"Hurry, Quig! Hurry! I can't hang on much longer." Tommy's voice was terribly frightened above the confusion of the water.

Quig couldn't hurry, he didn't dare hurry. If he fell and hurt himself, if he rolled into the water and was swept beyond his depth by the strong current, that would be all for both of them. There was no one else to do it.

"You *can* hang on, Tommy. You've *got* to, just a little longer!"

Quig forced all the strength he had into his voice, all the assurance. He hoped he sounded strong to the little boy waiting in the darkness, because at that moment he felt anything but strong himself. It was one thing to think about doing this, and another to do it. What had become of Peggy?

He slipped and fell a few feet, scraping his knees and his arms on the rough face of the cliff. He clutched wildly at a jutting rock, held still for a moment and then moved on toward the bottom. He couldn't have far to go now. Suddenly the child called out, "I see you, Quig. You're down."

Quig reached cautiously with his foot and felt water. He found that he was on a flat ledge of rock. He had done it, after all these years he had done it. But strangely there was no sense of elation. He just snatched off his slacks and shirt and sat down, gingerly sliding off into the river. The current caught him and he knew what was coming. Somehow he must find Tommy in that welter of tumbling water, and he must find him in time. He must wade as far as he could on the rocky bottom and pray that he wouldn't lose his balance and be flung down against the rocks. Also he must be constantly on guard against the deep holes that he knew were there.

"Here I am, Tommy," he called in as calm a voice as he could manage. "Hang on. Tell me which way to go."

Now that he had caught a glimmer of his brother's body through the darkness, Tommy began to cry. With Quig actually in the river, coming toward him, all of his bravery seemed to fade away. "I-I can't tell you," he sobbed. He snuffled mightily. "I've got water in my nose. I can't hang on any longer. I'm going to drown!"

The fear that had gripped Quig all the way down the bluff was transformed into blazing anger. "You sure are if you let go now, and you're going to drown if you don't keep talking to me so I know where to go. Stop that blubbering and *talk to me*, I tell you!"

"Come straight ahead," Tommy gulped, shocked back to control.

Quig saved his breath for struggling with the

current and inched his way over the rocks toward the sound of Tommy's voice. Once he slipped on a slimy stone and floundered into a deep hole, but a powerful kick sent him spinning to the surface.

"Here I am," Tommy squeaked in a very small voice, so close to Quig that he almost slid into another hole in astonishment.

"Let's go," Quig commanded, the strength generated by his anger still upon him.

The place where Tommy was clinging to the rock was indeed over his head, but Quig was so much taller that he could easily stand on the bottom. The water swirled around them dangerously, though, and Quig was anxious to get out of the rapids. He knew that the hardest part of the task lay ahead. Coming out by himself hadn't been so bad, but returning with a heavy, frightened child would be another thing. Quig braced himself against the current, supporting Tommy. His lifesaving instruction came back to him quickly.

"Now, Tommy," Quig said urgently, "you listen to every word I say and do exactly what I tell you."

"O.K., Quig, I will." The panic was gone from Tommy's voice now, and Quig felt sure he could count upon obedience. He floated him on his back, squatted down in the water himself, and flung Tommy across his shoulders. In a moment they were on their slow, perilous way to shore. As Quig

had feared, the going was very rough. His brother
was a solid, muscular seven-year-old, and Quig was
bearing his whole weight, with no water to lighten
the load. The footing was so precarious and the current so strong and erratic in the little rapids that
Quig wondered if he could manage even the few
yards he must go. Without Tommy to steer him
straight, it probably would have been impossible.
There was no sign of Peggy and the Munson children. He and Tommy were all alone in the empti-
ness of Dead End Bluff, struggling to get out of the
water.

Far away in the village Quig heard the wail of a
siren and wondered wearily where the fire was. He
slid into a hole and dunked Tommy. They both
came up spluttering. He heard the siren of the village squad car mingled with the sound of the fire
engine. They seemed to be coming closer, and Quig
thought vaguely, as he made the last part of his trek,
that the fire must be somewhere on Bluff Road.

Right now he didn't care. All he wanted in the world was to set Tommy down safely at the bottom of Dead End Bluff.

The water was shallower, the current pulled at him less savagely. A few more steps and he would have it made. Tommy had been unbelievably quiet all the way, but now he wriggled on Quig's shoulders and cried, "We're almost back!"

"Hold still," Quig ordered. "Don't upset the works now."

The wail of the sirens seemed to pierce the air above them, and then they were still, and Quig could hear the sound of excited voices, shouting at the top of the bluff. Above them all came Peggy's familiar, high call, "Quig! Are you all right? I've got help!"

She certainly had. As Quig's foot struck the shore and he crawled up onto the narrow little ledge it seemed to him that half the village must have come to the rescue. He heard the voices of Officer O'Brien and Officer Barry, plus the men of the volunteer fire department. He recognized Mike's deep voice and the higher pitched ones of Joe and Don. Liz and Joy must have come, too—he could hear their squeals.

"We're all right!" Quig called. "We're out of the water."

His first reaction was frustrated anger. Why did

she have to call out the police and the fire department, too? This was his problem, and he had solved it himself. Somehow, having all these people around took something away from him. In the first relief of getting back all alone, without help, he forgot that he had sent Peggy flying for aid, and that a little while before in the rapids he had wondered frantically what was taking her so long.

"Shine that spotlight right down the bluff, Mac," called Officer O'Brien to the captain of the fire department. "Now let's set your ladder up, and we'll get those kids up here in no time."

It remained for Tommy to set everybody straight as far as Quig was concerned. Standing in the glare of the spotlight, looking up at the dark bluff above them, he shouted in his high, childish voice.

"Nobody needs to come down here. I fell in the river, that's all, and my brother came down to get me and he carried me out. We can come up the bluff by ourselves."

There was a consultation at the top. Quig could hear them talking in low tones. What to do? He didn't really know, either. His inclination was to finish the job—to climb back up the face of the bluff with Tommy in front of him as he would have had to do if Peggy hadn't arrived with her rescue operation. On the other hand, his anger had cooled, and he realized that Tommy was very tired and certainly wasn't used to climbing around the bluff in the dark. He'd hate to insist upon bringing him up alone, just to look big, and have him fall and break a leg, or worse. There were chances you had to take, and chances you didn't.

While everybody stood pondering, there was the sound of a car rushing toward them on Bluff Road. The driver slammed on the brakes, and Quig heard the door flung open and numerous pairs of feet running to the top of the bluff. He heard his mother's voice with a frantic question, and Peggy explaining. Then his father's voice joined the conversation. Quig relaxed; they were home, and this was the time to leave the decision to them.

In a minute his father came to the edge of the bluff and called down.

"Quig, we've decided that the men will put the ladder down and bring Tommy up. As long as they're here, they might as well do it, and it'll be a lot easier."

The long ladder was lowered carefully over the edge of the bluff, and Mac came down. He settled it firmly at the bottom and said, "Come on, young one, let's go up. Quig, hold it for me, just to make sure, eh?"

He started up the ladder carrying Tommy, who protested every inch of the way. Quig waited, beginning to shiver in the cool of the August evening.

Mac had reached the top; Quig knew his mother had gathered her child into her arms when he heard her say, "Oh, Tommy!"

Quig began to search hastily around on the ledge for his pants and shirt, now that the crisis was over. He couldn't be sure where he had come ashore. To his great relief he came upon them and quickly scrambled into them. In the excitement of the moment he had forgotten that he was standing in the full glare of the spotlight in his underclothes, soaking wet. At any other time he would have been terribly embarrassed, but now it struck him as being hilariously funny and he began to laugh in fatigue and reaction to his ordeal.

"I'm coming down for you, Quig," Mac called.

"Oh, no, you aren't," Quig called back, suddenly serious. He would not accept help he didn't need. "If I can drag Tommy out of the rapids all alone, I guess I can climb this ladder by myself. Here I come!"

He climbed the ladder, slowly, carefully, but with perfect confidence. It was his father who waited at the top with firm hand to help him off.

"Well done, Quig!" he said.

"Thanks, Dad," Quig responded. "Next time I'll climb the bluff without the ladder."

Chapter 15

MORNING CAME WITH A FLEETING, TELLTALE CHILL of autumn in the breeze that blew into Quig's room. When he awoke and touched the braille numerals on his watch, he was amazed to discover that the morning was half gone. He hurried downstairs. Mother set his breakfast on the back porch in the sun, and his father came in from the yard, where he was working, to have another cup of coffee.

"Last night didn't seem to be the time to talk about what happened on Dead End, Quig," he began. "You were completely beat by the time we came home."

Quig laughed. "I can hardly remember a thing that happened after we left the bluff. I can't even remember going to bed!"

"You barely made it," his father said. "I thought I was going to have to put you to bed the way Mother did Tommy, but you finally roused enough to get undressed and crawl in."

His mother came out of the house and sat down beside him. "Tell us what happened, Quig—every single thing," she said. "When we drove up to Bradfords' and saw the fire engine and the squad car and the searchlight and all the people down at Dead End—well, you can imagine what I thought!"

So Quig began his story, trying to tell all the things his mother wanted to know. "I was a little bit to blame," he concluded. "I guess I told him once he'd probably have to catch his bullfrog at night. But when I said it, I never thought he'd go down there alone in the dark."

Mrs. Smith shivered in the sunshine and threw her arms around Quig.

"Oh!" she cried, "Just think what might have happened to both of you! I should have spanked him the minute he came up, but I just couldn't."

Quig sat still a second in the circle of her arms before he wiggled free.

"He didn't need it, Mom. He was scared stiff!"

"Helen," said Mr. Smith in a voice Quig hardly recognized, "I don't believe we ever have to worry again about this big one of ours. He showed more spunk and judgment last night than I've ever seen in any boy his age. I've never been so proud, Quig!"

All Quig could think of to say was, "Thanks, Dad!"

It was a feeble expression of his feelings. They were all silent for a while. Father sipped his coffee. Mother sat quite still beside Quig.

Then Quig began to speak again, "Something really happened to me on Dead End last night."

"Of course," his mother murmured sympathetically. "You're a mass of scrapes and bruises."

Quig brushed that aside. How could she, of all people, misunderstand!

"No, that's not what I mean. Dad, do you know how I've always felt about Dead End, ever since you told me never to go down the bluff?"

Jeff Smith hesitated briefly, and then he answered, "I'm not sure I do."

Quig walked over to the porch railing. "Well, Dead End has been a kind of symbol to me of all the dead ends in my life. Don't you see?"

"Yes, I think I do, now," his father said, thoughtfully.

Quig groped for words. "I think I learned something about all my dead ends last night. None of them will be easy, but now I think I can find a way out of most of them."

"Well, your going down Dead End did something for me, too," said his father. "Perhaps I've been one of your dead ends myself. Your mother thinks I've protected you too much. It won't be easy to change after all these years, but I'm willing to try."

Mother blew her nose and remembered a message for Quig. "George Munson called before you woke up," she said. "He's starting his vacation, so you won't need to go this morning, but Dorothy wants us all down for supper in the yard. It's Peter's birthday, and they're barbecuing a turkey."

This was the day that the elkhound breeder was expected in from New England to look at Viking, Quig remembered. It had been completely wiped from his mind. This was going to be a gloomy day, in spite of the hot August sunshine.

As it happened, however, he had little time to brood over the loss of Viking. Peggy came over to talk about last night. Quig's exasperation with her had died away by now, but he still thought the fire department was a little too much of a good thing.

"The police, yes, Peg. I can see that, but the fire department, gee whiz!"

"Well," Peggy explained, on the defensive, "I was so scared, and all the families on Bluff Road seemed to be gone, so I called the police, and then I thought that maybe the ladder would be handy to bring Tommy up the bluff, so I just called the fire department, that's all."

"I s'pose it was handy," Quig conceded reluctantly, "but it was kind of embarrassing."

Just before lunch Officer O'Brien, cruising by in the squad car, stopped to congratulate him on his rescue work. "Just like a professional!" he exclaimed admiringly. The neighbors had all heard about it by this time and stopped in to have Quig tell them the details himself. His friends arrived to sit on the front porch and hash over the whole thing a dozen times.

"Just think," said Mike, "we were all down in the park watching night baseball and might have missed the excitement. We followed the fire engine. Good thing Peg called it!"

They all went swimming in the afternoon and Quig had to tell his story to everybody they met. By supper time he was sick and tired of the whole thing and hoped he wouldn't even have to mention the subject that evening. He didn't need to worry. The breeder from New England had just departed as they walked through the gate at Munsons'. The Bradfords were arriving, and the yard was full of chatter.

Under cover of the noise Quig found George Munson and asked, "Did he want Viking?"

"He certainly did," Mr. Munson answered cheerfully, "and not only did he want Viking, but he was so impressed with Signe that he wanted her, too."

"Oh, no!" The protest came out involuntarily. He couldn't keep the words back. He felt the way he had last night when he was buffeted about by the water in the rapids. He finally pulled himself together and said,

"I thought maybe Signe wouldn't be sold until fall, and by that time I'd have saved enough to buy her." He managed a grin. "I s'pose that was just wishful thinking, though. I'll have to wait for two or three more litters before I'll have enough to pay for a registered elkhound. When's he going to take them?"

"He's on his way back to New England now, Quig," said Mr. Munson, gently.

"Oh!" Quig exclaimed. "I didn't even get to say good-by!"

"I'm sorry about that," Mr. Munson apologized, "but maybe it's better that you didn't."

Storm and Freya were barking frantically in the shed.

"Will you please let them out, Quig?" Mr. Munson asked. "I had to shut them in when the man left. They were so excited."

Quig went obediently to open the shed door, still stunned to think they were all gone. He had somewhat reconciled himself to having Viking go, but to lose Signe at the same time! He had hoped to have her at least until school started. He opened the door and the dogs surged out, whimpering their pleasure at seeing him. Suddenly, above their noise he heard the high whimper that he had learned to know so well during the last few weeks. He thought he must be dreaming, but the eager whimper went on, and he felt an insistent clawing at his leg. Unbelieving, he bent down, and Signe leaped into his arms.

Mr. Munson was beside him now, and Quig turned to him in complete bewilderment. "I don't get it," he cried. "Didn't you say that the man took both of them? What's she doing here?"

George Munson laughed. "You misunderstood me, Quig," he explained. "I didn't say he took both of them; I said he wanted both of them. I told him he could have Viking, but that Signe wasn't for sale."

"Signe isn't for sale?" Quig asked. The talk on the lawn had subsided now, and everybody seemed to be waiting to hear George Munson's answer.

"No. I've been watching her for quite a while, and I've decided that I couldn't possibly sell her. Once in a great while a puppy comes along that chooses a master, instead of the other way around. Signe is that kind and she's made her choice. Besides, I have other plans for Signe."

Quig held the puppy close in his arms and a great, wild, unreasoning hope leaped up inside of him. "What other plans?" he asked in a voice scarcely above a whisper.

Mr. Munson went on, and there was no sound but his voice and the whispering of the wind in the trees.

"You may remember that I offered a reward, and a generous one, when the puppies were stolen, to the person who could give us information about them. Surely you haven't forgotten what you heard on the night of the meet and what happened on your birthday, when we went to the island? I certainly haven't! If you hadn't heard the men talking and then if you hadn't smelled that woman's perfume and insisted that the Whitfords were there, we'd never have found them. It was your sharp hearing and your keen nose and your good memory, Quig, that got the puppies back for us. The reward is yours, boy. Will Signe be a suitable one?"

Quig was quite incapable of speech. He buried his face in Signe's deep fur and was grateful that nobody could see how he felt. With a tremendous effort he finally managed to answer.

"Will she be suitable? Gee! Mr. Munson, I don't know what to say. Gee, I never dreamed of anything like this."

Signe reached up and nuzzled his ear in her fa-

vorite way. George Munson clapped him on the
shoulder.

"I saved the reward until the day Viking went
away, to cheer you up a bit."

Quig turned his face toward Mr. Munson and
said clearly and firmly, for all to hear, "Let's get this
straight, once and for all. I don't give a hoot that she
isn't Viking. She's chosen me, and she's my dog."

George Munson chuckled with satisfaction.
"Good! I'm delighted that you feel that way. I kind
of suspected that that was the way the wind was
blowing."

The turkey was done, tables set up on the lawn,

birthday cake brought out, presents opened. Quig ate mechanically. Signe sat at his feet, and later he gathered her up onto his lap, and she snuggled there until it was time to go home. Mr. Munson came over and sat beside them and told Quig everything the famous breeder had said about his dog.

"He was really impressed, and would like to have had her. Said she was the best little female he'd seen all summer. When I told him what I planned to do with her, and why, he said, 'I predict the boy will be starting his own kennel with her one of these days.' "

His own kennel! What a great idea. Suddenly Quig wanted to take Signe home—to have her all to himself. The chill of an August evening was settling over them. His mother suggested that they had better go, and he was glad. Mr. Munson came out with a leash and a small choke collar.

"Here's Signe's wardrobe, Quig," he said, laughing. "I don't have to tell you to take good care of her. You do a better job with the dogs than I do. Bring her down tomorrow. She's not too young to learn a few basic manners."

Signe followed Quig happily home on the unaccustomed leash. She went upstairs with him to his room, and settled herself obediently in the box that Mother brought. Tommy came in to pet her before he went to bed, and the house gradually sank into its night stillness. Quig undressed and put on his pajamas, but he wasn't ready for sleep. He crawled under a blanket because the breeze was cool, but he lay wide awake, remembering the last two days, thinking of Signe, asleep in the box beside his bed, of Viking on his way to the new home in far away New England, of all the things that lay ahead for him.

A towboat hooted on its way down the Mississippi, and Tommy's big old bullfrog bellowed at the bottom of Dead End Bluff. Signe stirred in her box, he heard a scramble, and in a moment she wriggled her soft, warm body under the covers, and into his arms.

"You shouldn't be here, Signe," he whispered into her ear. "Mother wouldn't like it, but just for tonight, you can stay!"